_____

TO

_____

FROM

_____

DATE

CHRYSTAL EVANS HURST

100 DAYS TO

DISCOVERING
the
GIFT *of* YOU

A DEVOTIONAL JOURNAL

100 Days of Discovering the Gift of You: A Devotional Journal
Copyright © 2025 Chrystal Evans Hurst. All rights reserved.
First Edition, January 2025

Published by:

21154 Highway 16 East
Siloam Springs, AR 72761
dayspring.com

All rights reserved. *100 Days of Discovering the Gift of You: A Devotional Journal* is under copyright protection. No part of this book may be used or reproduced in any manner whatsoever without written permission except in the case of brief quotations embodied in critical articles and reviews.

Scripture quotations marked ESV are taken from the ESV Bible® (The Holy Bible, English Standard Version®) copyright ©2001 by Crossway Bibles, a publishing ministry of Good News Publishers. Used by permission. All rights reserved.

Scripture quotations marked NLT are taken from the Holy Bible, New Living Translation, copyright ©1996, 2004, 2015 by Tyndale House Foundation. Used by permission of Tyndale House Publishers, Carol Stream, Illinois 60188. All rights reserved.

Scripture quotations marked NKJV are taken from the New King James Version. Copyright © 1982 by Thomas Nelson, Inc. Used by permission. All rights reserved.

Scripture quotations marked THE MESSAGE are taken from THE MESSAGE, copyright © 1993, 1994, 1995, 1996, 2000, 2001, 2002 by Eugene H. Peterson. Used by permission of NavPress. All rights reserved. Represented by Tyndale House Publishers, Inc.

Scripture quotations marked TLB are taken from The Living Bible copyright © 1971. Used by permission of Tyndale House Publishers, Inc., Carol Stream, Illinois 60188. All rights reserved.

Scripture quotations marked NIV are taken from THE HOLY BIBLE, NEW INTERNATIONAL VERSION®, NIV® Copyright © 1973, 1978, 1984, 2011 by Biblica, Inc.® Used by permission. All rights reserved worldwide.

Scripture quotations marked AMP are taken from the Amplified Bible, Copyright © 2015 by The Lockman Foundation. Used by permission.

Scripture quotations marked CEV are taken from the Contemporary English Version. Copyright © 1991, 1992, 1995 by American Bible Society, Used by Permission.

Scripture quotations marked NASB are taken from the New American Standard Bible®, Copyright © 1960, 1971, 1977, 1995, 2020 by The Lockman Foundation. Used by permission. All rights reserved. www.lockman.org

Scripture quotations marked KJV are taken from the Holy Bible, King James Version.

Written by: Chrystal Evans Hurst
Content Collaboration by: Margot Starbuck
Cover Design by: Becca Barnett

Printed in China
Prime: U2772
ISBN: 979-8-88602-873-7

Have you discovered the gift of you?

If you're like many women I know, it's possible that you aren't yet entirely convinced that you are a one-of-a-kind wonder—a gift from God to the world.

And I get it. Maybe the last few decades just didn't unfold the way you once imagined. Or perhaps there was an unexpected rupture—a death, a medical challenge, a divorce—that you never expected. Or there may have been other obstacles that kept you from living the dreams you had for your life. I understand.

And I also believe that, starting today, you can embrace the gift of who you are.

So let me give you a glimpse of where I see us heading together on this one-hundred-day adventure together.

Because any effective strategy begins by assessing what's currently working and not working, that's where we'll start too. We'll take inventory, pausing to notice who and where you've been. And then I'll encourage you to be present where you are *right now*.

Next, I'll invite you to consider what's possible. You'll get to dream of who you want to be. And because we know that your best one-of-a-kind life is unique to who God has designed you to be, we'll explore that unique design together. We'll consider who God has made you to be.

After that, it's time to make a plan, set some goals, be strategic. And because we know that embracing the gift of you isn't done in isolation, we'll look at *who* is with you on this journey. Then we'll get a bit more specific about *how* to embrace what is most true—even choosing specific life-giving practices to support you in your commitment. Finally, I'll pick up my cheerleader pom-poms and cheer you on with a few more strategies for living well.

I know that you've been doing your best. I know that you wake up and make the most of each day that you're given. And I also know that who you are is worth naming and owning and celebrating. And I believe that embracing the gift of who you are is possible. I believe that, wherever you are today, you can discover the gift of you.

Let's do this!

Chrystal

NOTICE NOW.

A DIFFERENT LIFE IS POSSIBLE

*The counsel of the L ORD stands forever,
the plans of his heart to all generations.*
PSALM 33:11 ESV

I'd met a friend for lunch, and as we ate our salmon salads she shared with me how stuck she felt in her life. My friend (I'll call her Jen) was in her mid-thirties, and her life just hadn't unfolded the way she'd hoped it might. A decade earlier she'd imagined that she'd be married and a stay-at-home mom raising three kids. None of that had yet happened for Jen, and she was really disappointed with the life she was living.

Listen, I'm not going to lie. I kind of love having these conversations with friends and family—and now *you*!—because I have hope that when our lives aren't what we imagined, we are *not* stuck forever. I peppered Jen with questions, and by the time we left the restaurant, Jen had a bit more hope. Not only that, but we'd also crafted a specific plan of action that Jen would execute.

Over these one hundred days, I'm inviting you to discover the gift of *you*. Because God has created you for life that really is life, no matter what your reality looks like today, you can do this.

DAY 03

As you look at the lives of those around you, reflect on the people you know who have experienced God's blessing *later* than they expected.

_____
_____
_____
_____
_____
_____
_____
_____
_____
_____
_____
_____
_____
_____
_____
_____
_____
_____
_____
_____
_____

God, You have heard my cry. Even though I don't always understand Your timing, I am putting my trust in You today. Open my eyes as I sing a new song of praise to You. Amen.

NOTICE NOW.

THE LIE WE BELIEVE

Don't put it off; do it now!
Don't rest until you do.
PROVERBS 6:4 NLT

If you've ever been on a health-and-fitness journey, promising to begin eating healthier or exercising regularly, you may have had this thought: "I'll start tomorrow." *(Can I get a witness?)*

And when you said it, you really believed it. When you were polishing off your eighth slice of pizza or slurping down your "last" milkshake, you really believed that it was your final treat before you got serious about changing your life. Now, hear me, I'm not picking on you. I've been there. But I also want to name the sneaky lie that can get into our thinking. It's a lie that keeps us stuck: *"I'll do it later."*

Can you relate? We *know* what we should do, but we put it off. We let Grandma's sewing machine gather dust in the attic instead of asking a friend to teach us to sew. We haven't gone online to find the course schedule from the local community college. We haven't put together the résumé that would help us apply for the job we *really* want. We might even really believe that we'll "do it later," but "later" never comes.

Friend, tomorrow starts today. Now is the opportunity for you to start living. What's that thing that you know you should do but haven't done?

DAY 04

Ask God to show you that intention you've held in your heart that you've been putting off. Talk to God about what you need to do to pursue it *today*.

___

*Lord, I confess that I've been slow to act
on what I know I need to do. Please be my helper, now,
so that I can embrace all the goodness You have for me. Amen.*

NOTICE NOW.

YOUR BAD DECISION DOESN'T DEFINE YOU

Therefore, if anyone is in Christ,
he is a new creation;
old things have passed away;
behold, all things have become new.
2 CORINTHIANS 5:17 NKJV

Maria's parents always imagined that she would be the first person in their family to go to college. She'd always done well in school, and they'd been saving money for her education. But the week after high school graduation, Maria wrote her parents a note saying that she'd left to go on the road with her boyfriend's band. Fast-forward four years, and after Maria's boyfriend has left her for another woman, Maria is back living with her parents, working at a local grocery store. As many of her friends are graduating from college, Maria feels stuck.

There are all kinds of choices that Maria could make to begin to live a life she loves, but she has allowed her bad decisions to define her. While her family still sees all the potential in her, Maria can't get past the past. Sadly, she no longer believes that she's worthy of God's goodness.

Do you relate to any part of Maria's story? Is there something from your past that keeps you stuck? Beloved, I need you to hear that in Christ, the old is gone and the new has come. If you've asked God to forgive you, then *you are forgiven*! God has goodness in store for you, and today is the day that you can choose to receive it.

DAY 05

Notice anything from your past that may be keeping you from fully embracing the goodness God has for you today. Offer it to Him.

*Jesus, thank You for giving me a fresh start, beginning now.
I believe that in You I am a new creation.
Walk with me into the future You have planned for me. Amen.*

> NOTICE NOW.

CAST YOUR CARES ON HIM

*Let Him have all your worries and cares,
for He is always thinking about you
and watching everything that concerns you.*

I PETER 5:7 TLB

Have you ever felt bullied by your feelings? Have you held onto a negative emotion in such a way that it has kept you from embracing the gift of you? Negative emotions can take us so low that we struggle to find our way out. *So, what's a girl to do?*

First Peter 5:7 tells us to cast all our worries and cares on God because He cares for us. The word "cast" in this verse comes from the Greek word *epiripto*, a compound of the words *epi* (meaning on top of) and *ripto* (meaning to hurl or violently throw). God doesn't just tell us to trust Him with our worries. No, ma'am. He says violently throw them off of our own shoulders and onto Him.

When we live as if who we are is wrong, mistreated, and undervalued, that becomes our identity. So we start to give control to the very one who wronged us by living in a way that makes us puff our chests out, thinking, "They won't get one over on me! I have a right to be upset." But when we do this, we only hurt ourselves. We end up stuck in a mindset that traps us into believing (1) we are not valued, and (2) we have the right to allow hate to consume our hearts. But don't you think it's time to experience true freedom?

DAY 06

Cast your cares! Write down the recent occasions when your feelings took you out. Offer them to God and listen. Write down what you hear.

Loving God, I do believe that You care for me.
Today I am giving You my cares and concerns—I'm hurling them on You!—and I trust that You are receiving them. Amen.

NOTICE NOW.

A SHIFT IN PERSPECTIVE

"Look, dear son, you have always stayed by me, and everything I have is yours."
LUKE 15:31 NLT

As we're on the seventh day of this journey together, I want you to hear that God doesn't waste anything. He will take what was meant to cause harm and use it for good. If we follow His example, then we too can take the hard circumstances and find beauty in them. We simply have to shift our perspective.

You know the story of the wayward son? While his dad is living, this son takes his half of his inheritance and blows it on wild living. When he returns home, and his dad throws a party, his brother feels some kind of way about it. And when the older brother expresses his anger, the father offers him a shift in perspective. He says, "Look, dear son, you have always stayed by me, and everything I have is yours." The father reminded him, "You don't need a party. You already have everything."

And there *are* riches in every situation. Every relationship. You simply need to remember to pause, let go of the bad, and then be intentional about seeing the good. And as a heads-up: acknowledging the riches may challenge you to grow. It may move you to give more grace to someone than you would like, or forgive someone who hurt you deeply, or even see your own part in a bad circumstance. But trust me, friend, it is beyond worth it!

DAY 07

Yesterday you offered your negative emotions to God. Today, be intentional about finding the good. Write down the riches you find in your life today.

_____
_____
_____
_____
_____
_____
_____
_____
_____
_____
_____
_____
_____
_____
_____
_____
_____
_____
_____
_____
_____
_____

God, I confess that I don't always give You thanks for the riches in my life.
You assure me that everything You have is mine.
Open my eyes to all the riches You have provided for me. Amen.

NOTICE NOW.

PLANS TO PROSPER ME

"For I know the plans I have for you," declares the LORD,
"plans to prosper you and not to harm you,
plans to give you hope and a future."

JEREMIAH 29:11 NIV

After becoming a single mom during college, I worked hard to earn my degree and get that first job, but I wasn't happy. I hated my job. I hated being alone. And I didn't have any hope for what was to come. But you know what? The words of Scripture that my mother had spoken over me as a child rang in my ears: "For I know the plans I have for you. Plans to prosper you and not to harm you, plans to give you hope and a future." Guess what I did? I made a few lists. I made a list of things I couldn't change, and I made a list of things I could change. (Yeah, I'm a list girl.) Then, one at a time, I began attacking the things I could change. And I went from being the girl who was *struggling* to being the girl who has learned to push past obstacles to build a life I love.

Are there things in your life today that you just hate—maybe your job, your home life, a certain role you play, a weekly task? The good news is that there are things you can change and there is a way to push past your obstacles. In fact, God has plans to help you love your life again.

DAY 08

As you consider God's promise in Jeremiah 29:11, reflect on what it means today, *for you*, in light of your current situation.

Father God, I have faith that Your plans are to prosper me, giving me hope and a future. Today I put my trust in You, believing that You have good in store for me. Amen.

NOTICE NOW.

MOVING FROM DESIRE TO DECISION

I can do all things through Christ who strengthens me.
PHILIPPIANS 4:13 NKJV

Picture the volleyball team together in the locker room, right before the championship game. The coach is rallying the team, getting players psyched to play their best. And at the height of her pep talk, she asks, "How bad do you want it?" What that coach is asking is, "Do you want it badly enough that you're willing to pay the price to get there?" She's saying, "If it's in your power to do it, and you don't do it, then you don't want it enough!"

That's the question I'I m asking you today—"How badly do you want it?" Because if you don't want it badly enough, if you don't *really, really, really* want to create a life you love, you won't do the work to achieve it. You'll never move from desire to decision.

And *that*—moving from desire to decision—is where the magic happens. When you want to own your own home so badly that you forego going on that annual girls' trip, you've moved from desire to decision. When you want to meet a man to share your life with so badly that you visit the singles ministries in a few different churches, you've moved from desire to decision. And when you are so committed to breaking that bad habit that you ask a girlfriend to check in with you every day to make sure you're keeping your commitment, you've moved from desire to decision.

I believe that you can create a life you love, and I'm convinced that that happens when you move from desire to decision.

DAY 09

Identify one area in your life where you know you need to move from desire to decision. And be very specific about the decision you're making today.

_____
_____
_____
_____
_____
_____
_____
_____
_____
_____
_____
_____
_____
_____
_____
_____
_____
_____
_____
_____
_____

*God, I believe that because I have the power of Christ in me,
I can do all things. Strengthen me to execute the decision
I'm making today, for Your glory. Amen.*

NOTICE NOW.

VALUE IN STICKING IT OUT

*Let us not grow weary or become discouraged
in doing good, for at the proper time
we will reap, if we do not give in.*

GALATIANS 6:9 AMP

As we continue this journey to discover the gift of you, I want to offer one caution. Just because a situation in your life is challenging or uncomfortable, don't abandon it too quickly. Maybe you've been diligently saving money to take the trip of a lifetime, and you suddenly want to spend it all on a new car you don't need. Or perhaps a lifelong friendship has become pretty tricky. Or maybe you're just *tired* from taking the courses to earn your degree. When you look at your life today, it's not *feeling* like a life you love.

The reason I want to encourage you to stay with the saving and the friendship and the studies is because there is often *value* in doing hard things. If God is telling you to stick it out, then there's something you can glean from that situation. There is a way in which hard things grow us into the person God has designed us to be. So, while it would be easy enough to blow the bank account, ditch the girlfriend, or quit school, I believe that there can be something for you to gain from the situation in your life that feels hard right now. Let it teach you what it will teach you. I guarantee that if you stick it out, you will grow.

DAY 10

Look at the hard things in your life right now, and brainstorm the gifts or skills or strengths that can come out of them if you stick with them.

_____
_____
_____
_____
_____
_____
_____
_____
_____
_____
_____
_____
_____
_____
_____
_____
_____
_____
_____
_____
_____
_____
_____
_____

Gracious God, You know each of the hard places in my life right now, and I believe that You care. Grow me in these areas so that I might become the person You created me to be. Amen.

BE PRESENT.

PRACTICE GRATITUDE

Whatever is good and perfect is a gift coming down to us from God our Father, who created all the lights in the heavens.
JAMES 1:17 NLT

What will you be grateful for today?

In its simplest form, gratitude is the ability to recognize and acknowledge the goodness in your life. It is being thankful for what you have and what you've experienced. It is an appreciation for all things, tangible and intangible.

The truth is, you will have days when you simply want to have your bad day. You want to sit in that space and have a personal pity party. Do it! I am not telling you to never be in a funk. In fact, I am telling you the opposite. I want you to sit in your funk and let all those negative emotions out. Just know this—you cannot stay there! You can have your moment and feel your emotions, and then you have to let them go. Because as long as you try to hold them in, there is no space for gratitude.

I know that even the most grateful person has moments when life becomes overwhelming and gratefulness goes out the window. So, when we practice gratitude, we train ourselves not to sit in the negative moments. We acknowledge them, we process them, and then we find our way back to the positive.

DAY 11

Reflect on where you've been. Identify the moments over the years that changed you for the better. Give thanks for individuals who poured life into you.

*God, although my life isn't perfect, I give You thanks
for all the goodness I've experienced in my life.
Open my eyes today to see all the blessings You have given me. Amen.*

BE PRESENT.

NOTICE BEAUTY

*"All things were made through him,
and without him was not any thing made that was made."*
JOHN 1:3 ESV

Yesterday I invited you to notice what you can be grateful for in this season. Today I'm going to get a bit more specific. I want you to begin to be very intentional about recognizing the beauty that's around you.

When was the last time you stopped in your tracks to notice a sunrise or sunset? When did you crouch over a flower just to appreciate the way it was bursting with color? When did you pause to follow the slow path of a caterpillar making its way across the sidewalk?

There is plenty that you can be grateful for in your life, but some of it can be fleeting, right? We might not be able to afford the luxuries we'd like. There are seasons when our relationships get rocky. Professionally, we might not be exactly where we want to be. And that's exactly why I want to encourage you to tip your eyes toward the incredible unchanging beauty of what God has made. There is so much beauty and goodness in creation. Give yourself permission to take it all in: listen for the chirp of the bird outside your window or look toward a mountain range on the skyline or feel the rush of a cold stream.

Today, embrace the goodness of what God has made.

DAY 12

Spend time recording what you love to notice and appreciate in nature. And make a plan to enjoy it this week!

Lord, when You looked at everything You made, You called it good. And I do too! Help me to notice and give thanks for the undeniable goodness of all that You have made. Amen.

BE PRESENT.

BUILD IN MARGIN

*"Come to Me, all you who labor
and are heavy laden, and I will give you rest."*
MATTHEW 11:28 NKJV

In his book *Margin*, Dr. Richard Swenson noticed that he was seeing a lot of patients who were coming to him with similar symptoms, including fatigue and overload. After running tests on many of them, Dr. Swenson began to notice that the common denominator among those who'd been suffering was that they were all stressed out!

Many of us are running ragged. While our minds are occupied by checking things off our to-do list, our foot is on the gas pedal, and we're trying to keep ourselves from grabbing the phone off the dashboard to text the thing we're afraid we'll forget. Feel familiar?

If you're not intentional, distraction and busyness will come for you, and they will take you out. So, as you purpose to embrace the gift of you, I am encouraging you to build margin into your life. Maybe you choose to get up fifteen minutes earlier to just be *quiet* with God. That's margin. Maybe you choose to get really serious about not working on Sundays. That's margin. Maybe you block out three hours on Saturday to just *play* with your family and friends. That's margin. Be intentional about building it into your life,

DAY 13

Get really practical about identifying the places where you can build margin into your life. (Then put them on your calendar!)

Father, I believe that You created me to enjoy peace and rest. Teach me how to build margin into my life, creating a rhythm where I can be fully present with You, myself, and others. Amen.

BE PRESENT.

NOTICE THE DRIFT

*And I am sure of this,
that he who began a good work
in you will bring it to completion
at the day of Jesus Christ.*

PHILIPPIANS 1:6 ESV

"How did I end up here?"

Sometimes we have the very best of intentions to get someplace in our lives or accomplish something or achieve a thing, and it just doesn't happen. Then we wake up one morning and say, "I have no idea how I ended up here." I think I might know how it happened.

I call this phenomenon, this ending up far from where we'd hoped or imagined, "the drift." You feel me? Without ever intending to change directions, the experiences of life—our circumstances, the people around us, the choices we make, the influences we allow—can shift our course. We never made a decision to change course, and yet we wake up and notice that we are not where we imagined we'd be.

If that's you, you're not alone. And I'm going to name this moment as your opportunity to notice the drift and make a decision *today* to pivot. I'm not talking about just *desiring* your life to be different. I'm asking you to make a decision today to take steps to live a life you love.

DAY 14

Look for the drift! Consider all the areas of your life—family, friendships, work, education, leisure, faith—and identify the places where you've drifted. Then write out *the decision* you're making today to get back on course.

_____
_____
_____
_____
_____
_____
_____
_____
_____
_____
_____
_____
_____
_____
_____
_____
_____
_____
_____
_____

God, I believe that You intend to finish the good work
You've begun in my life. Give me courage to follow through
on the decision *I am making today to stay on course. Amen.*

BE PRESENT.

FOLLOW THE INKLING

For this reason I remind you to fan into flame the gift of God, which is in you through the laying on of my hands.

II TIMOTHY 1:6 NIV

Did you know that you don't have to see the whole big picture of what God has in store for you to begin living it?

When Paul writes a letter to Timothy, a young man he's mentoring, he's encouraging him to "fan into flame" the gift in him. He's telling him to *stir up* the gift of God that's in him. He's not telling him he needs a seminary degree or fancy letters behind his name to minister to folks. He's encouraging him to *just do it*. And that's what I'm encouraging you to do as well.

If you have an inkling about what God has for you, don't wait to see the whole big picture. Start where you are now. Maybe you love teaching people to cook. Invite a few teens from the neighborhood over and teach them to make your grandma's famous biscuits. Maybe you love to garden. Ask the elderly couple next door if you can plant something beautiful in their yard. Or maybe you've always wanted to write. Don't wait! Open up a journal or a laptop and write those words.

God is faithful to work with what we offer, so start right where you are.

DAY 15

Invite God to show you the "inklings" about how you might use your gifts to serve God and others. Brainstorm a list, and then choose one that you will embrace today.

*God, thank You for the gift of not having to figure it all out today!
Give me the wisdom and courage to begin where I am
and trust that You are leading me into the future. Amen.*

BE PRESENT.

DO THE NEXT THING

*In all your ways acknowledge him,
and he will make straight your paths.*

PROVERBS 3:6 ESV

Like many of us, my sister, Priscilla, imagined a different life than the one she has today. Specifically, she was taking the steps she needed for a career in television. But that's not where she ended up. She explains, "I was walking that path, and the Lord kept putting opportunities in front of me."

Whatever your plan has been, I want you to begin noticing the opportunities that God is putting in front of you. Maybe a woman at church has invited you to co-lead a small group with her. Or perhaps you won a contest for a scholarship to a weekend artist's retreat. Maybe you've always had a knack for working on automobiles, wanting to learn more, and you just inherited your grandfather's 1970 Dodge Dart. Notice the opportunities that are before you.

When it comes to discovering the gift of who we are, I know that everybody wants a formula. If you're one of those people, today is your lucky day. Because I think the formula is simply this: *do the next thing*. Priscilla agrees, "I did what was in front of me to do. I just kept doing the next thing. Now I'm standing in the middle of God's purpose."

DAY 16

What are some of the opportunities that God is putting in front of you in this season? List them and identify what your "next thing" will be.

___

*God, I am ready to walk with You.
Open my eyes to the opportunities You have put in front of me,
and give me courage to do my "next thing" with You. Amen.*

BE PRESENT.

TRUST THE PROCESS

*But if we hope for what we do not see,
we wait for it with patience.*

ROMANS 8:25 ESV

Imagine that your father is the CEO of a huge corporation, and when he publicly announces that he's planning for his retirement, he names you as his successor. Amazing, right? But the rub is that he doesn't rush into retirement. In fact, he waits fifteen more years! And during those years, you're still stuck cleaning toilets at headquarters. Bummer, right?

That's kind of what happened to David in the Bible. Except it was worse. After he was told he would rule and was anointed as king over Israel, he had to go back into the fields and care for his father's sheep for *fifteen more years*. That's pretty rough, right?

I believe that there was something for David in the midst of caring for the flock. I believe that God was doing something in him to prepare him to sit on the throne. And I also believe that there's something for you in the midst of whatever tasks are before you right now. When you look at your life today, there's something good for you to embrace, appreciate, and be thankful for. You just need to look for it. Look for the growth. Look for the beauty. Look for what God is teaching you.

DAY 17

Welcome God to shift your perspective on the way you're viewing your life today. Ask Him to show you what gems can be mined during this season.

*Loving God, give me the vision to see what You see
in my circumstances today. And teach me to be faithful
in the assignment You've given me for this season. Amen.*

BE PRESENT.

MAKE SPACE FOR YOU

"But when you pray, go into your most private room, close the door, and pray to your Father who is in secret, and your Father who sees [what is done] in secret will reward you."

MATTHEW 6:6 AMP

When Jesus taught the crowds how to pray, he encouraged them to go into their most private room, close the door, and pray. I kind of imagine that "private room" as a bedroom closet today. It's that place where we can be alone with God, and no one—not even a roaming toddler, a ringing phone, distractions, or dirty laundry—will find us!

As you continue to be intentional about being present in the present, I encourage you to make a space—in your home or even just in your heart—to spend time with God. If you can jet off to a tropical location for a spiritual getaway, do it! But all of us can choose to make room, right where we are, to be with God. Maybe it literally is your bedroom closet. There were seasons of my life when my space was sitting in my car. Or maybe you can find quiet space at a park or at the library.

Consider doing something special in that space you create to spend time with God. If your only option is to lock the bathroom door to keep everyone out, place a scented candle in there to create some ambiance.

Make room—physically and emotionally—to be with God in this season.

DAY 18

Get in the physical space you're creating and dedicate it to God. Get quiet and journal your conversation with God.

*Father God, I long to be in Your presence.
Please meet me in the physical space I've created to be with You,
and communicate to my heart. Speak, Lord. Your servant is listening.
Amen.*

BE PRESENT.

ENSURE YOUR TANK IS FULL

*Each day that we live, He provides for our needs
and gives us the strength of a young eagle.*
PSALM 103:5 CEV

Are you running on empty?

As you notice where you are right now and how you're moving through life, would you say that your tank is on "full" or is on "empty"?

If you're running on empty, it's likely your calendar is packed and you have very little margin in your life. If you're running on empty, you may be checking things off a list—at home or at work—but you may be neglecting the relationships that nourish you. If you're running on empty, it's possible you've put your relationship with God at the bottom of your priorities.

I want to share with you some of the things that fill my tank and invite you to consider what will fill yours. I certainly get filled and refreshed by spending time with God in Scripture and prayer. But I don't want to over-spiritualize this thing. I am refreshed by the glow of candles burning in my kitchen. I am enlivened when I turn on my favorite music (a little CeCe Winans and a little Celine Dion for the win!). I am energized when I get to share a meal with friends. I am fueled when I make time to read a great book. In winter, I'm energized by the cozy hug of a heated blanket. And you know what always replenishes my soul? A fifteen-minute walk outside.

This week, make the time to fuel your soul.

DAY 19

You heard some of the things that fuel me, and now I want you to brainstorm the things that fill *your* tank.

_____
_____
_____
_____
_____
_____
_____
_____
_____
_____
_____
_____
_____
_____
_____
_____
_____
_____
_____
_____
_____
_____

God, I've been running on Empty, and I long to be filled by You.
Help me make room in my life to receive from You
all I need to have a full tank. Amen.

BE PRESENT.

OPEN YOUR EYES

*"But blessed are your eyes because they see,
and your ears because they hear."*

MATTHEW 13:16 NIV

Have you heard those stories of the man and woman who started out as friends and eventually realized that they were made to be together forever? At the right time, God *opened their eyes*. Or have you ever dropped something small on the floor—a pill, a contact, a nose ring—and then had trouble *seeing* it to retrieve it? (Especially if it's the contact, am I right?)

Sometimes there is something right in front of us, and we don't see it. And that can be true for us as we purpose to build a life that we love with God. Maybe we loved to dance when we were younger, but we stopped dancing years ago. Or perhaps we're in the habit of offering rides to friends and neighbors and students and those from church who have special challenges, and we've never given it much thought. Or on occasion we might hit the craft store and get what we need to make a pair of earrings, and we are in our happy place.

I want to suggest that discovering the gift of you might be closer than you think. So turn on the music and dance. Embrace your call to "transportation ministry." Commit to making time to create once or twice a month. I want you to pay attention to what gives you life, and choose to walk in that way.

DAY 20

Make three columns: Past, Present, and Future. Remember where you've found joy in the past, notice where you're enlivened today, and even list the things you've meant to try but haven't yet embraced.

God, I long to see what You have for me,
and I confess I need You to open my eyes.
Show me where I might be neglecting the opportunities
that are right in front of me. Amen.

EMBRACE CHANGE.

ENVISION HEALTH

*Now may the Lord of peace Himself
give you peace at all times and in every way.
The Lord be with all of you.*

II THESSALONIANS 3:16 NIV

Here's a scenario to consider: When Jennifer was fired from her job as a graphic designer, after failing to meet a number of deadlines, she had been struggling with mental health issues. Without money to pay the rent, she sunk even lower. In fact, Jennifer spent most of her days at home, watching YouTube, without the energy to do much of anything, let alone hustle to get a new job.

Maybe you've had your own "low" seasons when you struggled emotionally. Maybe a life event—a death, a diagnosis, or a job loss—precipitated a hard season. Or perhaps, like Jennifer, your brain chemistry is such that you do have to be particularly vigilant about your mental health.

I want you to hear that you can choose to embrace health and wellness. You can make choices to eat foods that will nourish your body and your brain. You can make room in your day to exercise. You can turn off Netflix thirty minutes before bedtime to give your body time to settle. You can talk to your doctor about medication. You can seek the help of a therapist.

If you've wrestled emotionally, as so many have, you can choose to pursue health and wellness today.

DAY 21

Spend time with today's Scripture, from a letter Paul wrote, and ask God to point out the areas of your life where you don't have peace today. Invite God to transform those tender places.

___

*God, You are the Lord of peace. You made me,
and You know me inside and out. Be my helper as I embrace
a new way of living by choosing to embrace health and wellness. Amen.*

EMBRACE CHANGE.

BUILDING A STRONG BODY

She sets about her work vigorously;
her arms are strong for her tasks.
PROVERBS 31:17 NIV

Let's kick this devotion off with an inspirational story—one to consider as we dive into what it means to make the most of what God has given us: Jody, who used a wheelchair, was one of the strongest women in her group of friends. And not just "strong" in the sense that she was inspirational, which she certainly was. But I mean she was *physically strong*. She swam laps three times a week. She used her bulging biceps to transfer herself in and out of the chair. Once a week she was part of a dance troupe. And every month she went rock climbing at a local climbing wall! There were certainly ways in which her body didn't cooperate in doing all the things she would like to do, but she was a faithful steward of what her body *could* do.

As you consider what it's going to look like to discover the gift of you, I am encouraging you to make the best choices for your body.

The author of Proverbs describes the woman who has it going on in all areas of her life. I mean, in a moment in history when women were often expected to be subservient, she was a *boss*. And she was able to apply herself to all the things she had going in her life because she was physically strong.

All of our bodies have limitations, but we can choose to make the most of them when we prioritize investing in our health and wellness.

DAY 22

Consider how you are treating your body these days and how your body is treating you! Journal about any changes you'd like to make in order to *live well*.

*God, I believe that You knit me together in my mother's womb
and that You designed me to honor You with my body.
Help me to be the best steward of my body I can be, for Your glory. Amen.*

EMBRACE CHANGE.

HEALTHY SPIRIT

When I discovered Your words, I devoured them.
They are my joy and my heart's delight,
for I bear Your name, O LORD God of Heaven's Armies.
JEREMIAH 15:16 NLT

"The Lord is my shepherd."

"For God so loved the world . . ."

"Jesus wept."

If you have been intentional about feasting on God's Word, nourishing yourself with Scripture, those are a few verses that you might have tucked away in your heart. In fact, maybe they've been there since your childhood Sunday school days!

What about these days? Are you being an intentional student of God's Word? Are you nourishing yourself with the meat of God's Word, or are you content nibbling on junk food—like the inspirational meme you accidentally find on social media or some online video.

If you really want to flourish, I encourage you to pause and consider how you are feeding your spirit. Are you carving out time to receive the goodness God has for you? Are you intentional about memorizing Scripture, hiding it in your heart? To live your best life, nourish your spirit with what truly satisfies. If you need a place to start, you can choose to read through the Psalms in the Old Testament or choose a Gospel—Matthew, Mark, Luke, or John—in the New Testament. You got this!

DAY 23

Use your journaling time to write out the Scriptures that God brings to your heart and mind. If none come, open up your Bible and start eating.

_____
_____
_____
_____
_____
_____
_____
_____
_____
_____
_____
_____
_____
_____
_____
_____
_____
_____
_____
_____

*Father, I am hungry for You! Teach me to feast on Your Word
so that my spirit might grow healthy and strong.
Your words are my joy and my heart's delight! Amen.*

EMBRACE CHANGE.

GOD LOVES BEAUTY

*"And why do you worry about clothes?
See how the flowers of the field grow.
They do not labor or spin. Yet I tell you that not even Solomon
in all his splendor was dressed like one of these."*
MATTHEW 6:28-29 NIV

Let's start with a story that sheds light on why we should thoughtfully consider our living space: when Keyari found herself suddenly single after seven years of marriage, she leased an apartment near her workplace. Until then, Keyari and her husband had been living in a place that was already furnished. So as her friends helped her move all her things into the new apartment, she realized that during her marriage she had never made the space they shared feel like home. Keyari knew that for this season of her life it was really important to her to create a space that felt like a home where she could flourish. And so she purposed to make her new space one that delighted her soul.

As you are being intentional about discovering the gift of you, I encourage you to consider the space in which you live. Maybe you'll blow up some of your favorite photos from childhood and print them on canvases for your wall. Maybe you'll get a scented candle at the dollar store. When one friend of mine entered a season of life she wouldn't have chosen, she posted great big letters over her bed that announced: B-E-L-O-V-E-D.

When God adorned the fields with flowers, He *chose beauty*! I'm encouraging you to be intentional about your environment. It matters.

DAY 24

As you think about your environment, what features bring you joy?
And if you could change your space, what would you change?

*God, You are the author of all that is beautiful,
and You designed us to delight in beauty.
Show me how to live well in the space where I find myself today. Amen.*

EMBRACE CHANGE.

WORK IT OUT

*Also that everyone should eat and drink
and take pleasure in all his toil—this is God's gift to man.*

ECCLESIASTES 3:13 ESV

Have you ever looked at someone with an awesome job and dreamed that you'd be able to do what they do? Maybe you envied the Hollywood A-list celebrities shimmering in sparkly evening gowns on the red carpet. Or you might notice the woman running the Fortune 500 company who worked her way up from an entry-level position to being the CEO. Or you may just envy the girlfriend who's a freelance designer and gets to set her own schedule!

If you *love* the work you're doing now, give thanks to God for that. So many in the world don't have that privilege. And if you're unhappy with your job, spend some time journaling about changes you can make. Maybe you need to sign up to get a certification to move to the next level. Maybe when you put the kids down for bed at night you could use your evening hours to finally launch the side hustle you've been meaning to do for years. And maybe you just need to start sending out job applications!

With gratitude for whatever work you have right now, I encourage you to be intentional about the work that will pay the bills *and* bring you joy!

DAY 25

Notice the things you love about the work you do now—paid or unpaid!—and begin to dream of what you might put in place if you want to make a change.

Lord, help me to do my work—at home or in the workplace—to bring glory to You. And I welcome You to help me pursue the dreams that You have put in my heart. Amen.

EMBRACE CHANGE.

YOU'VE GOT A FRIEND IN ME

"Greater love has no one than this, that someone lay down his life for his friends."

JOHN 15:13 ESV

If you've lived in the same place for a long time and you are wired to build deep friendships, you may find that today your friendship plate is full! (If you've got morning coffee scheduled with one friend, lunch with another, and dinner with your childhood bestie, that's what we call a *full plate*.) But maybe you're the girl who's hungering for the kind of friend who you can share the deep stuff of your life with.

It's important that you hear me say very clearly that you're not a victim of happenstance when it comes to your friendships. Whether you're new in town or living in the community where you were born, you have a say in this thing! And while it can be easy to get stuck in self-pity if you don't have the friendships that you wish you had, Jesus' clear command can be our guide: "Love each other as I have loved you" (John 15:12 NIV). Rather than waiting for someone to come after you, take the initiative! Invite one of your coworkers out for dinner. Grab coffee with the woman at church you are intrigued by. Visit with the church mother who is homebound. You can be proactive to build the kinds of friendships that bring life to you and others.

DAY 26

Make two lists: In the first list, give thanks for the friends in your life, near and far. In the second list, begin to brainstorm those you can pursue.

Jesus, I am receiving Your command to love others the way that You love me. Guide my steps as I reach out to others with Your love. Amen.

EMBRACE CHANGE.

USE YOUR BRAIN

*And Jesus kept increasing
in wisdom and stature,
and in favor with God and people.*
LUKE 2:52 NASB

Do you remember the way it felt to finally be finished with school? Whether it was your high school diploma or your bachelor's or some other advanced degree, you might recall the wonderful freedom of not having a list of assignments and papers and tests hanging over your head! *It was awesome, right?*

But just because you may have completed your formal education, it doesn't mean that God doesn't want to keep developing your *mind*. In his Gospel, Luke announces that Jesus continued to grow "in wisdom and stature, and in favor with God and people." That's another way of saying that He grew intellectually, physically, spiritually, and socially!

Notice that first one. Are there ways in which you are making choices to grow *intellectually* in this season of your life? I'm not saying that you need to be doing research in a lab or solving complex equations, because, really isn't tipping a waiter fairly at a restaurant a complex enough equation? I'm suggesting that you can choose to grow intellectually throughout your life. It can be as simple as picking up a book from the library that interests you. Or maybe you'll choose to take a course at the local community college. In the hustle of our daily lives, it can be easy to forget to nurture our *minds*. Be intentional about your intellectual growth.

DAY 27

Review the ways that you grew intellectually in the *past*, whether it was formal education or self-guided learning. What type of intellectual adventure might light your fire today?

*God, I believe that You want me to be
a steward of the brain You gave me. Show me how I can
continue to grow intellectually in this season of my life. Amen.*

EMBRACE CHANGE.

HINDERING OR HELPING?

*Trust in the L*ORD *with all your heart,*
and do not lean on your own understanding.
PROVERBS 3:5 ESV

Today, ask yourself how the life you're living is helping or hindering you in the process of reaching your goals. Specifically, consider the events and people who are either helping you achieve your goals or hindering you.

Is the friendship that's basically built around wine and pricy appetizers at fancy restaurants helping or hindering you from reaching your goals? Is the habit that you just can't quit helping or hindering? Does the negative Nellie in your life, who always looks on the dark side of things, help or hinder? Does the way you use your free time help or hinder?

I'm encouraging you to notice what in your life today is helping you to embrace the gift of who you are and what might be hindering you.

I understand how easy it is to become discouraged when life doesn't seem to align with the dream you thought you were pursuing. But I want you to hear that as you take stock of your life today, you can make choices that equip you to get where you want to be!

DAY 28

As you consider where you want to be, in one year or in five years, make two lists: the "hinder" list identifies the things that could be hindering you from reaching your goals, and the "helping" list identifies the things that are pushing you forward in the right direction.

---

*Lord, I thank You for giving me the time and space
to reflect on where I am today and what You have in store for me.
Guide my mind and show me the best next steps. Amen.*

EMBRACE CHANGE.

WHEN THE GOOD ISN'T THE GREAT

All things are lawful [that is, morally legitimate, permissible], but not all things are beneficial or advantageous.
I CORINTHIANS 10:23 AMP

Sometimes a *good* thing isn't the *best* thing.

As you gear up to discover the gift of you, I've asked you to consider what could be hindering you from living out the dreams you have for your life. Maybe it's a person in your life or a bad habit or anything else that's getting in the way of the things you want the most.

But guess what? There also might be something holding you back that looks like a "good thing." And sometimes that's actually how we end up living a life we don't love.

Perhaps someone invites you to lead a Bible Study at church or organize a fundraiser for a nonprofit doing great work or mentor a troubled teen. And while those are "good things," they may not have your name on them. It's okay to consider something good and decide it's not for you. And that's why I'm giving you permission to begin to notice what does have your name on it and lean into those spaces.

When you are brave enough to release what is meant for others, you create space to pursue the life God designed just for you. In this season, purpose to say no to *good* experiences and people as you pursue your *great*.

DAY 29

Spend some time considering what "good" things in your life may be taking up room that was meant for great things. Offer these to God.

_____
_____
_____
_____
_____
_____
_____
_____
_____
_____
_____
_____
_____
_____
_____
_____
_____
_____
_____
_____
_____

God, help me to discern what is best.
Show me what, in my life, You're inviting me to release
so that I can be faithful about who You have called me to be. Amen.

EMBRACE CHANGE.

YOU CAN MAKE A CHANGE

*For we are His workmanship,
created in Christ Jesus
unto good works, for which God hath
before ordained that we should walk in them.*

EPHESIANS 2:10 KJV

We'll open this devotion with a narrative that demonstrates the power of embracing change: Sarah was having lunch with her coworker, Kiki, when she shared that she was disappointed with where she was in life. Sarah explained, "I just didn't think I'd be sitting at the same desk in the same cubicle a decade after I started at the company." Kiki had been hearing for months how dissatisfied Sarah was at work. Carefully, Kiki ventured, "You know you can do something about it, right?"

The look of surprise on Sarah's face signaled to Kiki that maybe Sarah *didn't* know that she didn't have to be stuck forever. Kiki continued, "You could talk to your manager about how you might get to the next level. You could take some continuing ed classes to build your skills. You could even polish your résumé and look for something you'd enjoy more."

Beloved, did you know that God created you for good works? That means that you were made to participate in God's good plan for the world and for *you*. I want you to hear clearly that you have the freedom to embrace change. If you feel stuck in your life—the way Sarah felt stuck in her job—you can make the choice today to change your circumstances.

DAY 30

As you consider the possibility of making changes to the life you're living today, how does that feel? Would you say you're hesitant or are you all in? Talk to God about it.

_____
_____
_____
_____
_____
_____
_____
_____
_____
_____
_____
_____
_____
_____
_____
_____
_____
_____
_____
_____

Faithful and loving God, I believe You created me for good things. Give me the courage to discern what I can do, and should do, to participate in that goodness. Amen.

IMAGINE POSSIBILITIES.

EXPECT GOD TO DO A NEW THING

*"Forget the former things; do not dwell on the past.
See, I am doing a new thing! Now it springs up; do you not perceive it?
I am making a way in the wilderness and streams in the wasteland."*
ISAIAH 43:18-19 NIV

Now that you've noticed where you are today and believe that you have the power to change your situation, you get to do the good work of imagining new possibilities.

In Isaiah 43, God announces, through His prophet Isaiah, "I am doing a new thing!" At face value, it almost sounds like a slogan for a greeting card, or a sentiment your grandmother might have cross-stitched on a throw pillow. But when God made this promise, the kingdom of Israel was divided and God's people were suffering. And that context makes God's promise so much more powerful for those of us who are hurting.

Maybe you've suffered the rupture of a marriage or friendship. Or perhaps you've lost someone you love. Maybe your work feels overwhelming. Or you might be grieving dreams of a husband or children or grandchildren. Precious friend, you can expect God to do a new thing. In fact, doing new things is what God is about. It's who He is. And it's why I'm so confident that God has good in store for you.

DAY 31

As you begin to imagine new possibilities, let God show you the "old things" that He is inviting you to release. Offer those to Him.

___

*God, You know every moment of my journey,
every ache, every loss. I offer these to You
with the confidence that You are doing a new thing. Amen.*

IMAGINE POSSIBILITIES.

GOOD FOR YOU

*And we know that for those who love God
all things work together for good,
for those who are called according to his purpose.*
ROMANS 8:28 ESV

As a child, you might have believed the possibilities for your life and who you could become were endless. Then, life *happened*, keeping you from investing in the reality of your hopes and dreams. You encountered your first heartbreak, a very real and painful disappointment. Perhaps there was an unmet expectation for how things should look in this season of your life. A difficult situation has caused you to question or redefine how God wired you. Maybe a bad decision has hindered you from honoring your life because of shame. Whatever the case may be, you've gotten off track with the plans that God desires for your life, and even more, you know you are not *staying true to the girl He designed you to be*.

This exploration is giving you the opportunity to remember that girl and imagine who she—and you!—can become. Your present does not have to be determined by the experiences of your past. It's not too late to get back on track with the girl in you! It's not too late to believe that a uniquely beautiful life is yours if only you will decide to live it. God has something in store for you, but it's going to take you responding to this opportunity to receive it.

Do you believe in your deep places that God is working good together for you?

DAY 32

As you imagine a good future, recall the girl you once were. What about that girl would you like for God to weave into who you are becoming today?

_____
_____
_____
_____
_____
_____
_____
_____
_____
_____
_____
_____
_____
_____
_____
_____
_____
_____
_____
_____
_____
_____

Father, I believe in my bones that I belong to You
and that You are working all things together for my good.
Show me who I am, in You. Amen.

IMAGINE POSSIBILITIES.

LIFE THAT REALLY IS LIFE

In this way they will lay up treasure for themselves as a firm foundation for the coming age, so that they may take hold of life that is truly life.
I TIMOTHY 6:19 NIV

In his letter to Timothy, the apostle Paul charges his young friend to command believers to do good and be generous. This, says Paul, is how to take hold of "life that is truly life." I love that language because I know that sometimes we can get stuck in a kind of life that's not quite living to the full.

When we spend hours every night on our couches binging Netflix, we may not be living life that is truly life. When we give in to the temptation to polish off an entire pizza and a pint of Ben & Jerry's Half Baked (#askingforafriend), we might not be flourishing in the way God created us to live. Or if we choose to harbor a grudge against a friend who wronged us, rather than forgive, we might not be choosing life that is truly life.

Friend, you were made for life that is truly life: doing good and being generous to others and to yourself. As you imagine the life God has for you, consider how it is one in which you are fully alive—doing good and being generous.

DAY 33

As you imagine what's possible, journal about a life in which you are doing good and blessing others. What might that look like for you?

___

Jesus, I believe that You made me to live life to the full.
Confident You forgive me for the choices I've made to live "empty,"
I put my faith in You to continue to lead me into life to the full. Amen.

IMAGINE POSSIBILITIES.

FILL YOUR SOUL

*"The thief comes only to steal
and kill and destroy;
I have come that they may have life,
and have it to the full."*

JOHN 10:10 NIV

You've got to brush your teeth. You need to do the laundry. And taking out the garbage when it's stinky? Well, that's another one of those nonnegotiables.

There are things in life we need to do that we might not love. But every day we can begin to make choices for things that fill our souls. No matter what requisite responsibilities we have—changing out our homes' HVAC filters or changing a baby's diapers or changing the oil in our car—we can also engage in soul-filling tasks that bring us life. We can make choices that help us to thrive.

For me, it's candles. I can choose to burn a linen-scented candle in the kitchen. For you it might be starting your day with a forty-five-minute walk with a friend. Or you might find life when you create colorful beaded earrings. One of the biggest mind shifts in this journey is really a simple one: you can *choose* to create a life you love.

Yes, you'll still need to get that garbage to the curb. But throughout the day there are countless choices you can make to live abundantly.

DAY 34

What are the little things that bring you joy? Make a big list and then commit to embracing one of those this week.

*Jesus, I believe that You came so that
we could have life to the full. Continue to show me
how to make little life-giving choices every day. Amen.*

IMAGINE POSSIBILITIES.

WELCOME GOD'S LEADING

For who can know the LORD's thoughts?
ROMANS 11:34 NLT

When I wake up, in the morning, there's one thing I try to do before I hit the ground running. (And, in fact, what I do is actually the *opposite* of hitting the ground running!) I lay there and reach for the sky. A wise woman once told me, "Stretch your arms toward every morning and say, 'God, I've got this thing I want to do today. But I want You to tell me what's most important for me in Your mind. Show me what You want me to get done with the time You've given me.'" So I just lay there and wait.

Sometimes God keeps it super simple for me: "Girl, don't forget to get the eggs from the store." And other times He might put a specific person on my heart to pray for that day.

As we're about a third of the way along this journey to discover the gift of you, I want to encourage you to continue to include God as your conversation partner in this process. As you ask yourself, "What could possibly be out there for me?" I also want you to be asking God the same question and listening for His voice gently offering that answer to your heart.

DAY 35

Write: *God, I want You to tell me what's most important for me, in Your mind.* Then journal on what you notice God speaking to your heart.

___

*God, Your plans stand firm and Your intentions can't be shaken.
I am hungry to hear Your voice so that I can be faithful
to live the life You have for me. Amen.*

IMAGINE POSSIBILITIES.

SAY NO— TO SAY YES!

"Let what you say be simply 'Yes' or 'No.'"

MATTHEW 5:37 ESV

Are you familiar with the power of *no*? We chatted a bit about making a deliberate choice to say no to some things in order to build margin into your life. But I want us to push even further to harness the power of no. Because if your plate is filled with too many yesses—*Yes, I'll drive someone to that event. Yes, I'll set up the room before small group. Yes, I can work the fundraising event. Yes, I can design that logo. Yes, I can make those calls.* There isn't room for the yes that has your name on it.

In order to create space to say yes to the thing that has your name on it, you have to exercise bravery to say no! And sometimes it really does take courage, doesn't it? It takes courage to say no to something that's a worthy cause. It takes courage to say no to something that you're gifted at doing. And it can take a *lot* of courage when you have to say that no to someone you love and respect: a friend, a parent, a pastor.

So this is me, encouraging you, to harness the power of *no*, because I'm convinced that it is exactly what frees you up to say a good solid yes to what God has for you.

DAY 36

Review the commitments in your life right now—and any others you might be considering—and ask God to help you sort them into those you should continue and those you can release.

_____
_____
_____
_____
_____
_____
_____
_____
_____
_____
_____
_____
_____
_____
_____
_____
_____
_____
_____
_____

Lord, I trust that You are the One who is guiding my steps.
Give me insight into what I can release, courage to do it, and the wisdom
to say yes to the opportunities with my name on them. Amen.

IMAGINE POSSIBILITIES.

FIND THE SILVER LINING

Consider it pure joy, my brothers and sisters, whenever you face trials of many kinds, because you know that the testing of your faith produces perseverance.

JAMES 1:2-3 NIV

When I need help to see something clearly—a situation in my life or a possibility I'm considering—one of the people I know I can turn to for godly counsel is my dad. And because he's a pastor, lots of other people turn to him as well! And when someone's kind of focused on what's wrong in their life, my dad might gently say to them, "I'll bet you're not looking at all there is. You're looking at the thing right in front of you. Tell me about something that's *right* in your life."

And it's not that he's trying to deny the reality of whatever it is that person might be facing. Rather, he's helping the person to build on the thing that's right in their life, because he knows we can train ourselves to see the silver lining in our situations. We can choose for optimism and against pessimism. So, he encourages the person to take off the glasses or the "lens" they've been using to view the thing, and put on a new pair of glasses that allows them to see a thing from God's perspective.

What is the situation in your life today in which you need God's vision?

DAY 37

Note the situations that you might identify as "dark clouds" in your life today, and invite God to show you the way He is viewing those things.

___

*Lord, I do count it joy when I face trials,
because I know it's building perseverance in me.
Give me Your vision to see what is* right *in my life today. Amen.*

IMAGE POSSIBILITIES.

COMMIT TO SELF-CARE

*Before daybreak the next morning,
Jesus got up and went out to an isolated place to pray.*
MARK 1:35 NLT

"Put your oxygen mask on first, before assisting others." The day our family was leaving for our vacation together, I would dip in and out of the boys' rooms to check what they were packing for the trip. They'd learned to lay out their folded clothes, organized day by day, and when they thought they'd nailed it, I'd check to see that they'd remembered everything they needed. Meanwhile, I was busy with work and making lunch and caring for my husband and paying those last bills before we left town. And when it was time for us to leave, *I hadn't packed for myself!*

A few hours later, after checking my quickly packed bag at the airport and boarding our flight, I heard the flight attendant on the plane say clearly, "Put your oxygen mask on first, before assisting others."

This isn't self-indulgent. In fact, Jesus would slip away, at the beginning of the day, to fuel up by being with His Father! Here's the thing, I need for you to practice self-care—to take care of *you*—so that you have the oxygen you need to care for others. Be intentional about packing your bags, ensuring that you've got what you need physically, spiritually, socially, and emotionally.

DAY 38

Talk to God about the areas of your life that you have let slide, for whatever reason, and how God might be welcoming you to practice self-care in this moment.

_____
_____
_____
_____
_____
_____
_____
_____
_____
_____
_____
_____
_____
_____
_____
_____
_____
_____
_____
_____
_____
_____

God, I believe that I am Your masterpiece
and that I am just as worthy of care as others are.
Teach me to value myself the way that You value me. Amen.

IMAGINE POSSIBILITIES.

HAVE A VISION

Where there is no vision, the people perish:
but he that keepeth the law, happy is he.

PROVERBS 29:18 KJV

The front of the City Hall building in Camden, New Jersey, erected in 1928, announces the words from Proverbs 29, "Where there is no vision, the people perish." What was true for the people of God who lived when Proverbs was written and what was true for the residents of Camden a century ago is true for us today.

If we don't have a vision for our lives, we'll never flourish. And yet when we investigate Scripture to discover God's vision—what God has to say about who we are!—we will begin to thrive. *Y'all, it works!* Let the truth become embedded in you until your soul knows it so intimately that you begin to live from God's vision of who you are.

Based on God's vision of who you are, what decision do you need to make for your life today? How could you decide to fight for your life? How might you move forward motivated to take claim of the abundant life that God has for you today (John 10:10)? When you consistently receive what God says is most true about who you are, you can begin to choose attitudes and actions that align with that vision.

DAY 39

Write down Scriptures that tell the truth about who you are! (Hint: if you're still learning the Bible, you can search online for "Bible, my identity in Christ.")

_____

Father, give me Your vision.
Let me see what You see when You look at me.
And help me to live from my identity as Your beloved. Amen.

IMAGINE POSSIBILITIES.

CHANGE IS GONNA COME

*Weeping may last for the night,
but a shout of joy comes in the morning.*

PSALM 30:5 NASB

The 1964 Sam Cooke song "A Change Is Gonna Come" is the narrative of someone who has suffered but believes that change is coming. In a haunting chorus, Cooke sings about how he has faced numerous hardships and setbacks, yet he remains hopeful and steadfast in his belief that a brighter future is on the horizon.

Maybe this is the song of your heart today. Beloved, I hope you're ready for the change that's going to come, because God is so faithful to deliver on His promise. In Psalm 30:5 the writer announces, "Weeping may last for the night, but a shout of joy comes in the morning."

Guess what? Morning is coming! If you have suffered, if you've longed for more, you can be confident that God has good in store for you. I am convinced that God is in the business of revitalizing our lives in a way that brings joy to us, joy to others, and joy to God. And I believe that *now* is the moment God is going to do a new thing in *your life*.

DAY 40

What has been that heavy thing—an event, a season, a grief, a burden—that lasted in your life for a night? As you release it, ask God to prepare your heart for what's coming next.

___

God, I trust that You are the One who makes all things new. Today I release the old and welcome what You have for me, next, with a shout of joy. Amen.

DISCOVER STRENGTHS.

ONLY ONE YOU

*You created my inmost being;
You knit me together in my mother's womb.
I praise You because I am fearfully and wonderfully made.*
PSALM 139:13-14 NIV

In all the world, there never has been—nor will there ever be—someone *just like you*. It's kind of mind-blowing, right? You are a divinely inspired work of art. Beautifully and carefully designed, you are unrepeatable. You are a unique combination of emotional wiring, intelligence, gifts, interests, and personality. There are things that leave you in awe, or give you the giggles, that other people wouldn't even notice. There are even things that make you furious that are unique to you! And along with your precious uniqueness comes the responsibility of being a steward of this life you've been given.

Go ahead and imagine God's fingers knitting you together in your mother's womb. And as God is crafting you, He is giving you arms and legs and eyes and ears to do just what you were designed to do. He is creating you to be in relationship with Him and with others. He is imagining the lives you will touch and the one-of-a-kind purpose you will have in His kingdom.

In this section of our journey we're going to dig into the unique *wonder* you are as you consider what you were made for. And that *wonder*-fullness begins with the fact that God designed you as one-of-a-kind in all the earth.

DAY 41

Close your eyes and imagine God's fingers crafting you in your mother's womb. Use your prayerful imagination and let God show you what He envisioned for you and your life.

___

God, I marvel that I am precious to You and unique in all the world. Open my eyes to what You intended for me and to my role in Your kingdom. I am yours! Amen.

DISCOVER STRENGTHS.

YOU ARE CHOSEN FOR A PURPOSE

*"You did not choose Me but I chose you,
and appointed you that you would go and bear fruit."*
JOHN 15:16 NASB

Remember when you were a kid and you wanted desperately to be chosen for something? Maybe you wanted on the kickball team at recess. Or maybe you tried out for cheerleading or soccer in middle school and you hoped you'd be picked for the team. And then in high school, as you were applying to colleges, you wanted to be selected by your top school choice. And eventually you may have wanted that special guy to look your way.

Dr. Curt Thompson says, "We all are born into the world looking for someone looking for us." *That's powerful, isn't it?* We want to be seen, to be known, to be heard, and to be understood. We want to be *chosen*.

Beloved, you have been chosen by the One who made you and loves you. And Jesus says, specifically, "I chose *you*." And He continues to name the reason we were chosen. (Spoiler alert: It's not to win games, or hype up the fans in the bleachers, or even to succeed academically or socially.) Jesus says that you were chosen in order to *bear fruit*. And the kind of fruit He's describing is to love one another.

You were born looking for someone to look for you. Be assured that God sees you. God chooses you. And God equips you to bear fruit by loving others.

DAY 42

You were made to love and be loved. Reflect on your journey of "looking for someone looking for us"—both your looking for a human person and a divine one.

_____

*God, thank You for seeing me and for choosing me.
Equip me to be the kind of person who does the thing
I'm made for: love You and love others. Amen.*

DISCOVER STRENGTHS.

DIFFERENT GIFTS

*We have different gifts,
according to the grace given to each one of us.*
ROMANS 12:6 NIV

My oldest child—grown now, with children of her own—is Kariss. And when she was eight or nine years old, I took her with me to the seamstress. When we arrived, the seamstress gave my girl a needle and thread to keep her occupied. Well, a few weeks later Kariss had created something. Was it something easy, like an eyeglasses case? No. Was it a sleeping bag for a stuffed animal? No. One day my girl announced, "Mom, look at my dress." And wouldn't you know it, Kariss had created this off-the-shoulder fitted dress with this long dipping tail in the back. Isn't she amazing? So, it won't come as a surprise that Kariss went to school for fashion design. The giftedness in Kariss made itself *known*.

Friend, just as that gift was knit into Kariss, there is a gift that God has put in you. It may not be the creative kind, like Kariss was given. Maybe you are someone who's a really good listener. Or perhaps you're one of those smarties for whom schoolwork came easily. Or maybe you are gifted as a servant and are generous in the ways you care for others.

I am inviting you to begin to notice the kinds of unique gifts God has given you so that you can be a good steward of those gifts.

DAY 43

Make a robust list of all your gifts! If you get stuck, invite someone who knows and loves you to chime in. (Don't be shy. This list is just for you!)

_____
_____
_____
_____
_____
_____
_____
_____
_____
_____
_____
_____
_____
_____
_____
_____
_____
_____
_____
_____

*God, I believe that You have given me gifts
that I am called to use for the good of Your kingdom.
Open my eyes to know how I can use them for Your glory. Amen.*

DISCOVER STRENGTHS.

PAY ATTENTION

Now there are varieties of gifts, but the same Spirit;
and there are varieties of service, but the same Lord;
and there are varieties of activities, but it is the same God
who empowers them all in everyone.
I CORINTHIANS 12:4-6 ESV

Okay, while we're on the subject of the gifts of the women I love more than anything in the whole world, I'll tell on my sister Priscilla. (If you know her, nothing about this will surprise you.) When Priscilla headed off to college, my dad advised her to major in communications. You know why? He knew she liked to talk a lot! Truly, that girl has *always* had something to say. And Priscilla has continued to be a faithful steward of those natural gifts as a speaker and an author.

I want you to stop to listen to the people around you—from your girlhood until today—who have had eyes, like my dad, to *recognize* your giftedness. Maybe your grandma recognized that you were a gifted chef in the kitchen. Or perhaps your friends are in awe of the handbags you make. Or it could be that there was that one teacher who took a special interest in you and really made you believe that you were a mathematical genius.

A lot of times the gifts God has given us are plain—if not to us, then to those around us!

DAY 44

Spend some time reflecting on the "noticings" that others—family, friends, teachers, mentors, coaches, guides—have had about your special giftings.

God, I confess that sometimes I can make this business of becoming the woman You made me to be harder than it needs to be! Open my eyes to the gifts You've put in me. Amen.

DISCOVER STRENGTHS.

I CAN LEARN TO DO IT

*God has given each of you a gift
from His great variety of spiritual gifts.
Use them well to serve one another.*
I PETER 4:10 NLT

Do you know the difference between gifts and abilities? In my opinion, your gifts are inherent in the way you were made, and your abilities are the kinds of skills and tasks you can learn to do. For example, while Kariss is incredibly creative, she had to learn to operate a sewing machine. She had to learn to use a serger. And now she has those abilities. And while Priscilla is a natural communicator, she has honed her skills as a writer. She's *developed* that ability. I was always a numbers girl, but I didn't know how to do taxes until I went to school for it.

Sometimes we have to invest time and energy into growing our gifting or developing a skillset. So, I want you to begin to imagine what that might look like for you. Maybe you'll finally save your dollars and attend a writing conference. Or perhaps you'll ask a neighbor who's a master gardener to teach you how to make things grow. Or you might check out some books from the library that teach you how to be the entrepreneur you know you were born to be.

As you begin to sense a direction God is leading you, determine what abilities you need to do that thing, and invest time, energy, and possibly dollars into developing those abilities.

DAY 45

You likely have some sense of the gifts that you've been given, so now spend time noticing both the abilities that you have developed—that equip you to maximize those gifts—and also the ones you may *need* to develop.

Lord, I believe that You can and will strengthen me to grow in the abilities I need to do the thing for which You made me. Show me what those are and give me the grit to stick with them! Amen.

DISCOVER STRENGTHS.

WHEN HEART AND FLESH SING

My soul longed and even yearned for the courtyards of the LORD; my heart and my flesh sing for joy to the living God.

PSALM 84:2 NASB

The writer of Psalm 84 describes what it is to live with a passion for God, saying, "my heart and my flesh sing for joy to the living God." And I'm wondering if you've had that experience before—of your heart and flesh *singing*? It may be that you've had that experience in a holy encounter with God. But we can be passionate about other things as well. And that passion that we have? It has to do with how we're uniquely designed by God.

For example, I *love* music. And if I hear a song with a great drumbeat, like Superstition by Stevie Wonder. Well, it's all over. I am passionate about that song. It makes my heart and flesh *sing*. That kind of passion is what sets your soul on fire.

So, what is it for you? And don't limit your imagination. My mom was passionate about beautiful sunsets. Someone else is passionate about the exact ratio of oils and seasoning to make the world's best popcorn. One woman is passionate about seeking justice for the oppressed. And someone else's heart and flesh sing when they get to dance salsa!

The fact that God gave each of us distinct passions tells me that those passions are integral when it comes to creating a life you love. What makes your heart and flesh sing?

DAY 46

This is a fun one! Make a list of everything that brings you great joy. Go big or go home. Ask God to remind you of all the things about which you're passionate.

*God, I am choosing to own the unique passions
that You have given me. And when my heart and flesh sing,
I will give praise to You! Amen.*

DISCOVER STRENGTHS.

KNOW HOW YOU'RE MADE

Do you have the gift of speaking?
Then speak as though God Himself were speaking through you.
Do you have the gift of helping others?
Do it with all the strength and energy that God supplies.
I PETER 4:11 NLT

I have a friend who knows that she's an introvert. But because she's great onstage with a microphone in her hand while speaking to thousands of people, some of her friends don't believe her! One day my friend stumbled upon an article naming the facts that many introverts actually do shine on stage, naming how very different that is than the stress of having seventeen interactions at a cocktail party! (Yes, she felt very vindicated.)

I think that personality tests, like Myers-Briggs or StrengthsFinder, can be so helpful in teaching us about the way we've been uniquely designed by God. And it gets you one step closer to designing a life you love. Because when you know how you're naturally wired—introvert or extrovert, thinker or feeler—it helps you to discover the gift of who you are. It doesn't mean that your introverted self will never have to attend another exhausting party or that your extroverted self will never need to practice thirty minutes of death-dealing silent meditation. What it does mean is that when you have those experiences, you will know how to recharge your battery! And you can make choices to lean into the nature that was God's unique intended design for you.

DAY 47

If you know results from a personality inventory you've taken, reflect on those. If you don't, find one online! Then consider what adjustments, if any, you want to make in your life as a result.

God, I celebrate the fact that You designed me to be unique in all the world. Teach me how to engage well in the world because I know who I am and how I am. Amen.

DISCOVER STRENGTHS.

KNOW WHO MADE YOU

*You made all the delicate, inner parts of my body
and knit me together in my mother's womb.
Thank You for making me so wonderfully complex!
Your workmanship is marvelous—how well I know it.*

PSALM 139:13-14 NLT

Sometimes it can be tempting to look at ourselves and be *critical* of what God has made. (Amen? I know it's not just me.) Really, God, with the ADHD? And why would you make me with limited vision? What exactly were you thinking with these hips? And the anxiety? Really, God?

The psalmist is convinced that God is the One who made us, and I'm going to believe that an intentional God had a purpose when He made me. And when He made you. I don't pretend to understand God's intentions, but if I use my prayerful imagination, I can perhaps begin to explore what God might possibly have had in mind. For example, I've heard that folks who aren't neurotypical, or have other types of physical or emotional challenges, can have a tender heart for those who face their own challenges. I'm not going to pretend to know why some folks struggle with anxiety or depression, but I *do know* that God is very present to those who know they need Him.

Your one-of-a-kind design by God likely includes some incredible gifts and passions, and it also may include some challenges. And I'm confident that God can use those challenges for your good and for the good of others. Ask God to show you how.

DAY 48

Consider the ways in which you have been *critical* of how God made you. Then, one by one, offer those to God and ask God how *He sees* each one.

God, I believe that You are the One who made me, **on purpose.**
*Give me Your vision for the parts of myself I don't yet love,
and show me what You have in mind for me. Amen.*

DISCOVER STRENGTHS.

WHAT WE'VE BEEN *READIED* TO DO

Let the redeemed of the L*ORD*** tell their story.**
PSALM 107:2 NIV

When Tiffany's birth mother got pregnant as a sixteen-year-old, it was hard to see what good could come of that hard season. Although Tiffany was adopted into a family that loved her, she struggled with feelings of rejection and abandonment throughout her childhood and young adult life. With the help of a therapist and some incredible prayer warriors, God graciously healed Tiffany's hurting heart just before she met the man she'd marry. When Tiffany and her husband adopted a daughter, God used both the tender spots in her own heart and also the healing He'd done in her to bless and nurture that little girl that He loved.

I am thoroughly convinced that God can and does use all the experiences in our lives—the good and the bad, the painful and the pleasurable—for the sake of His kingdom.

Beloved, your journey is entirely unique. It is like no other. So, I encourage you to notice the unique experiences you've had, and open your heart and mind to imagine how God might want to use those today in your life.

DAY 49

Write down a list of experiences that are unique to you. (For example: *I never knew my dad. I was born missing an arm. I was the valedictorian of my high school class.*) Offer each one to God and let Him show you how He can use that experience for good.

_____
_____
_____
_____
_____
_____
_____
_____
_____
_____
_____
_____
_____
_____
_____
_____
_____
_____
_____
_____

God, I believe that all my experiences have readied me for the plan You have for me and my life. Show me how You will use all my experiences to bless others, in Jesus' name. Amen.

DISCOVER STRENGTHS.

NURTURE *YOU*

"Since you are precious and honored in My sight, and because I love you, I will give people in exchange for you, nations in exchange for your life."

ISAIAH 43:4 NIV

The world will tell you one of two things: give until you give too much at the expense of your own well-being, or hold back and selfishly consider yourself above all else. Neither one sounds quite like God's good plan for you, do they?

Part of understanding your unique contribution to the world is valuing the gift of who God created you to be and stewarding that gift well. I want to continue to encourage you to own the responsibility of taking care of you by intentionally loving yourself and stewarding your life. Through the prophet Isaiah, God announced to His people, "You are precious and honored in My sight, and . . . I love you." And I want you to be treating the person who is precious to God—you!—with tender care.

You've begun to consider your gifts and abilities and interests and nature, and I want you to stick with that exploration. This week, carve out time to take note of what makes you, *you*. What sets your soul on fire? What sparks creativity and passion? What relaxes you? What fills your cup? What is refreshing and replenishing to you? What might you need to let go of? What might you need to add to your life? This week, make room to care for you.

DAY 50

You have your marching orders: take note of what makes you *you*. (You've already begun this inquiry. Use this exercise to gather all you've learned.)

___

God, because I am precious to You, I will treat myself as precious and worthy of care. Just as I've committed to steward my gifts for others, show me how to care for myself. Amen.

DEVELOP STRATEGY.

MAKE A PLAN

*Commit to the Lord whatever you do,
and He will establish your plans.*

PROVERBS 16:3 NIV

Are any of these on your list of goals for your life?

- I want to compete in the next winter Olympics as a figure skater.
- I want to be the smartest woman on earth.
- I want to climb Mount Everest before I die.

Go big or go home, right? *Well*... we're in the part of our journey now where I want you to be setting some goals for yourself. And they don't need to be Mount Everest-sized goals at all. (Phew!) And I really want you to be SMART about these goals.[1] I want the goals you're choosing to have five particular qualities:

- Specific
- Measurable
- Achievable
- Relevant
- Time-Bound

We'll unpack these together, but I want to launch by encouraging you to choose some goals that are *doable*. You know what's doable? Drinking four extra glasses of water every day. That's doable. Choosing to spend fifteen minutes with the Lord before getting out of bed? Doable. Pulling out your watercolors twice a month and painting? Doable.

In this section of our journey, you'll be making some practical, doable goals that help you to discover, *and love*, the gift of you.

---

[1] https://en.wikipedia.org/wiki/SMART_criteria

DAY 51

Consider times in the past when you've set a goal for yourself and failed. As you consider the SMART way to make goals, consider which aspect may have contributed to the fail. Identifying an area of weakness is the first step in developing your strengths.

*God, I know You are with me on this journey
and I continue to commit all my plans to You.
Give me wisdom to discern and to choose well. Amen.*

| DEVELOP STRATEGY. |

BE SPECIFIC

"If you are faithful in little things, you will be faithful in large ones."

LUKE 16:10 NLT

To set the stage for our devotion, here's a story that highlights key aspects of goal-setting: I decided," Macaiah announced to her husband, Jonathan, one morning as she rolled out of bed. "I'm going to be fit! That's my goal." Jonathan wanted to be supportive, but he felt confused. "What does that even mean?" he asked. "I mean, is it like taking vitamins? Completing a marathon? Is it eating leafy green veggies every day?" Jonathan knew something about goals that Macaiah didn't yet know: for goals to be achievable, they need to be *specific*.

There's no confusion about goals that are specific: *I will practice the guitar for thirty minutes, six times a week. I will learn to make my mom's lasagna and serve it to my family in the next fourteen days. I will finish the book I'm reading by Sunday night.*

I hope this feels like good news to you! If you've struggled in the past with making goals and keeping them, it might have been that you weren't specific. After a raucous night of sweets and alcohol, you may have announced on January 1 that you were going to lose weight in the new year. If that didn't happen, it may have been because your goal wasn't specific. Maybe you want to stop eating each night after seven. Maybe you want to find the perfect painting for the living room. Write it down; make it happen.

DAY 52

To whet your appetite for goal making, I invite you to write down five goals that are very specific and then choose one to execute. (Hint: to have goals that serve the whole person, you might consider these broad categories: physical, mental, social, emotional, spiritual.)

_____
_____
_____
_____
_____
_____
_____
_____
_____
_____
_____
_____
_____
_____
_____
_____
_____
_____
_____

God, I believe that You care about the little things in my life. As I seek to be the person You made me to be, I'm committing to You the small goals I'd like to accomplish. Amen.

| DEVELOP STRATEGY. |

MEASURING UP

*Commit your way to the L*ORD*,*
trust also in Him, and He shall bring it to pass.
PSALM 37:5 NKJV

Remember that sample goal I dropped a few days ago: "I want to be the smartest woman on earth"? I was playing. I think there are several things that are problematic about that particular goal, but the biggest one is that it's not measurable. Now, if you wanted to be the *tallest* woman on earth or the *heaviest* woman on earth, those are both *measurable*.

This is likely obvious to you already, but when you set a goal that's not measurable, you never know if you've achieved it. Whether you're aiming to be the best driver in your state or the funniest person at your high school reunion, those goals aren't possible to evaluate because they're not measurable.

As you've spent time considering your giftings and abilities and interests and nature, what spark ignited inside you? Maybe it was your passion for all things music-related. Or it might have been that you're a really funny person. Or it could be that you remembered you've always wanted to write poetry. Choose a measurable goal for one of the strengths you noticed in those areas: *I'm going to start taking piano lessons. I'm going to show up to perform at open mike night next Monday. I'm going to write one poem this weekend.* When your goals are measurable, they're doable.

DAY 53

With your gifts, abilities, interests, and nature in mind, create *three* goals that are very "specific." Choose one to execute this week.

_____
_____
_____
_____
_____
_____
_____
_____
_____
_____
_____
_____
_____
_____
_____
_____
_____
_____
_____
_____

God, thank You for guiding me as I consider
all You've put inside me! Grant me the diligence
I need to be a person who achieves what she purposes to achieve. Amen.

DEVELOP STRATEGY.

BELIEVE IT, ACHIEVE IT

You've all been to the stadium and seen the athletes race. Everyone runs; one wins. Run to win.
I CORINTHIANS 9:24 THE MESSAGE

When Diana Nyad decided to swim from Cuba to Florida—as a woman in her sixties!—many doubted that the goal was achievable. And for the first several attempts, it was not. But in 2013 Nyad completed the 110-mile journey through sometimes treacherous waters. Nyad never doubted that her goal was achievable.

The kinds of goals you want to be setting are ones that are *achievable*. If you rush into this goal-setting like a bull in a china shop, you might commit to goals that aren't *likely* achievable: performing on the piano at Carnegie Hall, playing quarterback at the next Super Bowl, or becoming a billionaire before you turn fifty. While I commend you on your ambition, these aren't goals that are likely to be achievable.

Achievable goals are more like: taking piano lessons or joining a coed touch football league or deciding to set aside two hundred dollars a month into a savings account. Achievable goals are those at which you are likely to succeed! I think that dreaming big is commendable, but if you don't identify a goal that's achievable, you'll only end up feeling frustrated.

DAY 54

Look back at the three measurable goals you listed in the last devotion. Of the remaining two, identify the one that is most achievable, and *go for it*! Spend time reflecting on how you'll succeed at this goal. Be specific.

*Lord, thanks for joining me on this journey.
And thank You for opening my eyes
to see where You're leading me. Amen.*

DEVELOP STRATEGY.

STAY RELEVANT

*I will instruct you and teach you
in the way you should go;
I will counsel you with my eye upon you.*

PSALM 32:8 ESV

Let's imagine that you're a visual artist. An oil painter. There are some goals that you might choose to establish for your success. For instance, visiting The Louvre in Paris might be on your bucket list. Or taking a painting class from a successful local artist might be a goal of yours.

Then there will be other goals—noble ones, worthy ones—that are going to be less effective at equipping you to discover and embrace the gift of you. For instance, if you want to succeed as an oil painter, then being able to run a mile in under six minutes isn't likely a goal that will serve you well.

And while that's fairly obvious, I want to push a bit further. Maybe you sorta kinda want to go scuba diving in Hawaii. But the most important thing in the whole world to you is finishing your memoir. Rather than Hawaii, consider renting an Airbnb during your week of vacation and making progress on the memoir.

Goals that are relevant to the life you most want to be living are the ones that will serve you well.

DAY 55

Pause to identify five things you'd like to achieve in the next decade. And when you can point to the one that matters most to you, then commit to a goal relevant to that success that you'll execute in the next thirty days.

_____
_____
_____
_____
_____
_____
_____
_____
_____
_____
_____
_____
_____
_____
_____
_____
_____
_____
_____
_____

Lord, I believe that You can and will strengthen me to grow in the abilities I need to do the thing for which You made me. Show me what those are, and give me the grit to stick with them! Amen.

DEVELOP STRATEGY.

TICK TOCK

*Teach us to number our days,
that we may gain a heart of wisdom.*
PSALM 90:12 NIV

Maybe you're one of those people who's announced that you want to climb Mount Everest before you die. Kudos to you! I don't want to burst your bubble, but when I think of those I know who've lived into their eighties and nineties, not one of them was going to climb four flights of stairs, let alone Mount Everest. If you don't get specific about when you'll achieve your goal, you're less likely to succeed.

Physical decline aside, research shows that those who make goals that are time-bound are 40 percent more likely than their peers to succeed!

That's big, right? So use it to your advantage. I'm encouraging you to put a timeline on your goals. Choose one or two that you can achieve in the next ninety days. And if you're really committed to Mount Everest? Put a date on that goal. Whether it's that you'll make plane reservations in thirty days or you'll execute the hike in twenty-four months, you'll be most likely to succeed if you set a schedule to achieve your goal.

DAY 56

Mount Everest was big, right? Don't be intimidated by that beast. Maybe you want to watch a sunset at the beach. Or replace a lightbulb in the basement. Offer some goals—from baby lightbulb ones to big beach ones—and put a time frame beside each one.

_____
_____
_____
_____
_____
_____
_____
_____
_____
_____
_____
_____
_____
_____
_____
_____
_____

*God, You are the One who has numbered my days.
Teach me to be wise with the ones You've given me!
Guide me as I chart the way forward to achieve the goals
You've put in my heart. Amen.*

| DEVELOP STRATEGY.

KEEP GOING

"But as for you, be strong and do not give up, for your work will be rewarded."

II CHRONICLES 15:7 NIV

If you've ever made a New Year's resolution, and especially if you abandoned that resolution by January 13, you may know what it's like to feel defeated when you fail to achieve your goals. Maybe you decided to finally learn to crochet. Or you committed to learning German. Or perhaps you chose to run a marathon. But for all kinds of reasons, you may not have achieved the goal you set for yourself. Sister, don't let past failure stop you today! People who set goals are ten times more likely to be successful. So there's real value in pausing to name your goals.

I also want you to hear that the January 13 fail does not have to be the end of the thing. Too often we get in a headspace where one setback causes us to abandon our pursuit of the goal entirely. It's almost as if we let ourselves off the hook because we stumbled! Instead, I want you to be giving yourself grace, whether you succeed or have a setback. And when you do falter, I'm giving you permission to reassess and get back in there.

DAY 57

Jot down some times from your past when one stumble would cause you to abandon the goal you'd set for yourself. How can you approach your goals differently now?

_____
_____
_____
_____
_____
_____
_____
_____
_____
_____
_____
_____
_____
_____
_____
_____
_____
_____
_____

Lord, You are the One who has called me to do good,
and I believe You are the One who can sustain me.
Give me endurance to achieve the goals I set. Amen.

| DEVELOP STRATEGY. |

ENDURANCE WINS THE RACE

God blesses those who patiently endure testing and temptation.

JAMES 1:12 NLT

When James wrote a letter to Jewish Christians, which we find in the New Testament, it was probably about AD 45. And that means it was about a dozen years beyond the death and resurrection of Jesus. Now today, we have the hindsight to know that we're still waiting for Jesus' return, but in the first century, believers wouldn't have had any idea what the timeline would be!

And so James is writing to many who've been hanging on to their faith, sometimes in very difficult circumstances, and he's encouraging them to keep going.

I'm wanting you to think about setting both short-term and long-term goals for yourself. So let's consider goals you want to set to stay healthy spiritually. A short-term goal you might set would be to read all one hundred fifty psalms over a ninety-day period. That's doable. And it may be that you also set a long-term goal. If you're someone who's struggled with alcohol abuse, you might commit to not drinking a single drop of alcohol again. That's the definition of long-term! And if that's you, I want you to receive James' words, and God's blessing, for those "who patiently endure testing and temptation."

Choose some goals that are short-term and others that are long-term.

DAY 58

Ask God to show you what goals He is calling you to make that are long-term and those which you can achieve in a shorter period of time. Brainstorm many, write them down, and then choose one of each!

_____

*God, I give You thanks that You knit me together in my mother's womb and You will stay with me until I meet You in glory.
Sustain me in these days and in the many that are to come. Amen.*

DEVELOP STRATEGY.

UNIQUE TO YOU

Your hands have made me and fashioned me; give me understanding, that I may learn Your commandments.

PSALM 119:73 NKJV

Do you ever feel exhausted by friends who set and achieve these lofty goals? It's that girl who announces she's going to run a marathon (#guilty!) or the one who successfully launches her own business or the one who welcomes half a dozen foster kids into her home.

I want to suggest the possibility that those might be exactly the right goals for them. But I want for your goal to be *unique to you*. And the principle, or filter, I want to offer you today is a simple question: "Does this help me live a life I love and was created for?" For a lot people who might consider the race, the business, or the extra kids, the answer could be no.

What's the goal you need to set that's going to help you embrace the life for which you were made? Maybe it's as simple as deciding to walk to the library once a week instead of driving. Or it might mean that you make room every weekend to do the craft that brings you joy. I want for the goals you choose to aim for to be uniquely aligned with who you are.

DAY 59

As you glimpse back over the last few decades of your life, what were the experiences in which you were absolutely *thriving*? What were the experiences—the hobby, the serving, the surprising friendship, the work—in which you felt fully like yourself? And how will these guide the goals you'll make today?

_____
_____
_____
_____
_____
_____
_____
_____
_____
_____
_____
_____
_____
_____
_____
_____
_____
_____

Father God, I am the work of Your hands.
Thank You for making me unique in all the world.
Continue to teach me how to become the person You created me to be.
Amen.

DEVELOP STRATEGY.

WHATEVER YOU DO...

Whatever you do, work at it with all your heart, as working for the Lord, not for human masters.

COLOSSIANS 3:23 NIV

In his letter to the church as Colossae, Paul exhorts his listeners to do everything with all their hearts, and I want to extend the same challenge to you when it comes to setting and reaching your goals. Yes, you're going to keep your eyes on the finish line—whether that's literally the finish line of a 5K or it's launching your online side hustle. But in order to make it to the finish line, I want to encourage you to be faithful in the small things.

Maybe you can imagine a world where you're selling the jewelry you make online. But there are little baby steps you need to take to get you there—and making the jewelry is just one of them! You've got to build a website or create an online store. You've got to figure out how you're going to reach potential customers. You may need to advertise. (You may need to find someone who knows how to do those things! Keep reading, because that's where we're headed together.)

The key to reaching the finish line is to take one step. And then the next one. And then the next one. Be faithful, moment by moment, to do the small things necessary to reach your goals.

DAY 60

In this section you've considered and set a few goals for yourself. Choose one of those and consider what "baby steps" you'll need to take to make it to the finish line. List them all here.

_____
_____
_____
_____
_____
_____
_____
_____
_____
_____
_____
_____
_____
_____
_____
_____
_____
_____
_____

*God, I confess that I can get distracted by the big thing
and neglect doing the smaller things You ask of me daily.
Give me the wisdom and courage to take the baby steps. Amen.*

ENGAGE OTHERS.

WHAT MATTERS MOST

*A friend loves at all times,
and a brother is born for a time of adversity.*
PROVERBS 17:17 NIV

My grandmother had eight children, and at the end of her life she was cared for by her youngest daughter. My grandmother was grateful for her children and that they cared for her so well. I suspect you've heard the same thing I have: When people are at the end of their lives, none of them wish they'd spent more time at work; none wish they'd hustled a little harder to make more money; none count the fancy house or car as being very important at all. At the end, what matters to most people are *relationships*. And when those who are dying *do* have regrets, they wish they had invested more into their relationships.

Relationships are going to be a big part of *discovering the gift of you*. If you want to have a life you love, invest in your relationships. Rather than sleeping in, get up on Saturday morning to do breakfast with a girlfriend. Do a video call with an old friend who lives across the country. And if you want to get really crazy—and I hope you do— write and send a card to someone you love.

Nurturing your relationships is a key ingredient to discovering the gift of you.

DAY 61

In different seasons of our lives, God places different people in our lives. Spend time making a list of the precious relationships—family and friends—whom God has given to you over the years. Then make an action plan to connect.

_____
_____
_____
_____
_____
_____
_____
_____
_____
_____
_____
_____
_____
_____
_____
_____
_____
_____
_____
_____
_____
_____

God, You have gifted me with family and friends,
and I recognize the ways You've loved me through them.
Help me to love them the way You do. Amen.

ENGAGE OTHERS.

TWO

*The heartfelt counsel of a friend
is as sweet as perfume and incense.*
PROVERBS 27:9 NLT

Picture a little girl on a playground running up to another little girl on the swings, flashing a bright smile, and exclaiming, "Let's be friends!" It's beautiful, isn't it? Whether you were the extroverted girl making the announcement or the introverted one who welcomed it, doesn't it seem like friendship is just easier for kids than for grown women?

A few years ago, the surgeon general of the United States declared loneliness an epidemic. In fact, nearly half of Americans reported that they only had three friends or fewer. In an age where we seem to be connected—digitally—to everyone, making authentic connection can feel a lot trickier.

No matter how old we are, we need our sisters! Yes, we need them to learn how to bake sourdough or to find the best places to shop for the cutest clothes. But we also need these friendships in our lives when the bottom falls out: when the diagnosis is received, when the marriage ends, when the child dies. We need each other in good times and bad. God created us to share life in community, and our lives are richer when we operate according to His good design.

DAY 62

Mapping out your life, year by year, note the names of the ones who have been your "girlfriends," at age six and age fifty-six! Give God thanks for these women, and then follow up by sending one a card expressing your gratitude for her.

God, I believe You made me for community and that friendship is a gift from You. Thank You for the girls and women You've placed in my life. Teach me to love them well. Amen.

ENGAGE OTHERS.

TWO ARE BETTER

*Two are better than one,
because they have a good return for their labor.*
ECCLESIASTES 4:9 NIV

When you're little, you spend hours every day with friends: on the walk to school, during recess, in the backyard, or cuddled up inside sleeping bags. In high school, you may share time together during cheerleading practice or track meets or church choir practice. And on college campuses? Dorm life is a great place to build friendships with other young women. But what about the years when you're launching your career? Or beginning a marriage? Or raising kids? Or caring for an aging parent? It can get trickier to nurture our relationships, can't it?

You've now paused to notice the girls and women who've been your friends *over the years*. But what about today? What do your relationships with women look like today?

If you're satisfied with the friendships in your life today, let's pause and thank God for that good gift. (#ThankYouJesus!) But maybe your relationships aren't as robust as you'd like them to be. I want to encourage you to spend time considering why that might be and committing to rectify it. Beloved, even if you feel stretched thin these days, *this is where you want to invest*! You were created to be in relationship—with God and with others—and friendship is a critical piece of discovering, and embracing, the gift of you.

DAY 63

Consider the friendships in your life today, both the number of them and the quality of them. Which relationship will you nurture this week? And if your friendships today aren't robust, who will you pursue, with care and kindness, this week?

God, You did not create me to walk this life alone.
Thank You for the friends You have given me.
Teach me how to best invest in the women in my life. Amen.

ENGAGE OTHERS.

THE FRIEND WHO SHARPENS

*As iron sharpens iron,
so one person sharpens another.*
PROVERBS 27:17 NIV

There are some friends, the ones we smile at and wave to in church or the ones we make small talk with at parties, who we may not *go deep* with. They won't know when our marriage is difficult. They won't know when we're having surgery to remove fibroids. They won't know when we're aching over a family member's addiction. And that's okay.

When we look at the life of Jesus, we see that He had concentric *circles* of relationships. There were seventy-two followers He sent out to share the good news. There were twelve in whom He invested His time and energy. And within that dozen were three—Peter, James, and John—who were *closest* to Jesus.

It's okay that you're not dishing about your gyno-surgery at the Pastor's Anniversary Lunch. But you do need to have people with whom you can share the intimate details of your life. And Proverbs 27:17 announces, "As iron sharpens iron, so one person sharpens another." That means that there are friends who make us better. They push us to make an appointment with a marriage counselor. They drive us to and from surgery. They comfort us when we're sad. Invest in the kinds of deeper friendships where you are sharpening and strengthening one another.

DAY 64

Not every friend tells us the honest truth or pushes us to be better. Think about those friends in your life who have truly *sharpened you*. Who are those friends and how have they showed up for your life?

_____
_____
_____
_____
_____
_____
_____
_____
_____
_____
_____
_____
_____
_____
_____
_____
_____
_____
_____

God, I'm not interested in shallow relationships.
I want to go deep with a few friends, making them better
and being made better by them. Bless these friendships, Lord. Amen.

ENGAGE OTHERS.

HAVE A MOTLEY CREW

And let us consider how to stir up one another to love and good works, not neglecting to meet together, as is the habit of some, but encouraging one another, and all the more as you see the Day drawing near.

HEBREWS 10:24-25 ESV

Now that I have hopefully convinced you that you *need* friends, I want to spend some time talking about the *types* of friends you need. I am not suggesting that you have to "cast" these roles of friendship or only accept certain people into your circle based on your current vacancies, but I want you to know that we can't expect a single friendship to fulfill our every need when it comes to connection.

Just like Jesus had that motley crew of twelve, we need a variety of friends who will speak into different aspects of our lives. And when we start to cultivate different relationships that may offer us different perspectives, we will see our souls grow in ways that we never imagined. One friend is going to be the girl who delights in you and makes you feel like the queen you are. Another friend is the one you'll turn to when you're really sad, because she knows how to be present with pain. And another one will be your first phone call when your cheating boyfriend you spent four years with breaks up with you! This friend will be filled with righteous anger!

Again, these aren't roles you have to "cast," but do notice the wonderful variety of different ways your friends care for you, based on who they are.

DAY 65

A few days ago, you considered the friendships you have today. As you review those, jot down here what unique gifts those friends bring to your relationship. (And also consider what you offer them!)

_____
_____
_____
_____
_____
_____
_____
_____
_____
_____
_____
_____
_____
_____
_____
_____
_____
_____
_____
_____
_____

Lord, just as You made me to be unique in all the world, You also made my friends to be unique. Thank You for the special gifts each of them offers to me and to the world. Amen.

ENGAGE OTHERS.

FOR SUCH A TIME

Yet who knows whether you have come to the kingdom for such a time as this?
ESTHER 4:14 NKJV

If you're not familiar with the book of Esther in the Bible, it's a doozy! Esther was born a Jew, and later in life she's chosen by the King of Persia to be his bride. And when her people are at risk of genocide, Esther boldly speaks up, at great risk to herself, to save them. Pretty awesome, right?

And if you read the whole story, you'll notice that there was someone in Esther's life who was her "hype man." It was a member of her family, Mordecai. Esther was orphaned as a girl, and Mordecai raised her. And when she's put into this position of great authority, he's cheering her on. He's whispering in her ear. And he's telling her that she was created and called "for such a time as this." He's telling Esther that she has this important purpose.

Do you have a friend like Mordecai? A friend who is just certain that God has appointed you to do a thing *and* that you'll succeed at it? I hope you *do* have a friend like this. Whether or not you've got this cheerleader in your corner today, guess what? You can be this friend to someone else. You can purpose to recognize the unique gifts they bring to the world and shake your pom-poms, encouraging them to be the woman God made them to be.

DAY 66

Reflect on the people in your life who've insisted, "You have a purpose" and "You can do this." Note the ways they've inspired and encouraged you. (And mark your calendar to encourage a friend in this way this week!)
If you haven't had a friend in your life who supported you, use your journaling time to write a prayer asking God to meet the need for authentic connection in your life.

___

Lord, thank You for those in my life who inspire me
to live as an agent of Your kingdom.
Show me how I can be that friend in the life of others. Amen.

ENGAGE OTHERS.

WE ARE FAMILY

*"Honor your father and your mother,
that your days may be long
in the land that the Lord your God is giving you."*

EXODUS 20:12 ESV

One of the ten commandments announces, "Honor your father and your mother, that your days may be long in the land that the Lord your God is giving you." For that instruction to make the "big ten" signals that it's *pretty important*, right? It is. It really is.

And in some families, like mine, it's not hard. My folks made it pretty easy for me and my siblings to want to honor them. I'm not saying we always did it perfectly, but because of who my parents have been, the commandment *makes sense*.

But maybe you didn't have a mother who spoke Scripture over you or a father who was steeped in God's Word. You may have even endured neglect or abuse at the hands of the people who should have cared for you. If that's your experience, I'm so sorry. I know that relationships with family—whether parents or siblings or aunties and uncles or cousins—can be tricky. But as you welcome God to help you design a life that delights Him, and delights you, this needs to be a piece of the puzzle. So spend some time talking to God about this and seeking His guidance for your relationships with family.

DAY 67

One by one, list your family relationships and offer each one to God, listening for His counsel. Who is He asking you to forgive? Who is He asking you to move toward? Where is He suggesting you create some healthy distance? Pray, speak, listen, respond.

God, I offer my family to You. As I seek Your healing and purpose to be emotionally healthy, guide my steps. I need Your help to walk well within my family. Amen.

> ENGAGE OTHERS.

INVESTING IN OTHERS

*Walk with the wise and become wise,
for a companion of fools suffers harm.*

PROVERBS 13:20 NIV

Okay, here's a fun party game: What do Moses, Elijah, and Deborah have in common? (Imagine the *Jeopardy* theme song playing while you're considering the answer.) Yes, they were all prophets, but all three of them were also leaders who mentored the developing leaders who followed behind them. For instance, Moses encouraged and taught Joshua. Elijah coached and inspired his successor, Elisha. And Deborah poured into an army captain named Barak. So as they were leading others, these three were also investing in those coming behind them.

As we think about crafting a rich life, we can look to wiser, more experienced mentors who've walked the path ahead of us. Maybe it's that older woman at church whose faith inspires you to grow closer to the Lord. It might be a supervisor at work who is shepherding you as you grow. Or it could be a neighbor who has raised children who are thriving and who coaches you as you parent your own kids.

We weren't created to do life alone. And so, at every age, we look for these older, wiser mentors who are willing to invest in us. (If you're further along the road and might mentor another, keep reading!)

DAY 68

Whether or not you've had a formal mentoring relationship in your life, list those who have invested in you throughout your life, and give God thanks for them.

_____
_____
_____
_____
_____
_____
_____
_____
_____
_____
_____
_____
_____
_____
_____
_____
_____
_____
_____
_____
_____

*God, I thank You for those who have poured life
into me on my journey. In this season,
show me who I can follow and learn from. Amen.*

ENGAGE OTHERS.

BE A YODA

These older women must train the younger women.
TITUS 2:4 NLT

One of the most iconic mentoring relationships of all time is the one between a little dude named Yoda and a young Jedi named Luke Skywalker. But there are others! For instance, did you know that Meryl Streep mentored Viola Davis? And even Oprah Winfrey—who's invested in so many people over the years—was mentored by Maya Angelou.

Now, I'm not sharing this so that you can go get yourself a Yoda, a Meryl, or a Maya. No, now I'm suggesting that you are called to be the Yoda, the Meryl, or the Maya in the life of another. Before you get stressed out, let me take the pressure off. When you mentor someone, you're not giving them something you don't have. Quite the opposite. When you invest in others, you're sharing what you've learned on your journey. So if you're a published author, you might coach another writer who's seeking publication. Or if you're a woman in business who's been successful at smashing the glass ceiling, you can share your experience with a recent business school grad who's beginning her career. Or if you've walked with the Lord for decades, you can invest in a younger woman who has recently given her life to Jesus. Who is it that you can invest in, in this season?

DAY 69

I know it can feel like a lot to identify as a mentor. So let's break it down. Make a list of your experiences—with God, with education, with work, with recovery, with emotional healing, with all the things you can think of. Then ask God to show you who might benefit from the particular wisdom you bring.

---

*God, I confess that I don't always feel like a Yoda.
But I trust that You've called me to invest in others
and that You'll provide all I need. I put my trust in You, Amen.*

ENGAGE OTHERS.

SURPRISING FRIENDSHIPS

But if anyone has the world's goods and sees his brother in need, yet closes his heart against him, how does God's love abide in him?
I JOHN 3:17 ESV

As we've considered the kinds of relationships that can make life good—those with friends and family and mentors and mentees—I want to throw one more type of relationship into the mix that makes life good.

And I'm just going to name these "surprising" friendships. It's the authentic friendship between a woman who's financially wealthy and a woman who lives in a government-subsidized apartment building. It's the sweet friendship between a ten-year-old boy and the elderly man who lives all alone next door. It's the deep, abiding friendship between a black man and a white man. It's the genuine relationship between the Ivy League grad and her neighbor who lives with an intellectual disability.

I know that these types of relationships are part of the good life because I see surprising relationships like this in the life of Jesus. And while our modern eyes and ears could easily miss them today, they were radical in His culture! It's His conversation with a woman at the well who was considered to be the wrong race, wrong religion, and wrong gender! It was the way He socialized with those His culture considered to be "sinners." It's the surprising ways He treated children and women with dignity and respect.

To live well, discover the rich goodness in these surprising Jesus-style friendships.

DAY 70

Consider the people in your everyday orbit: walking in your neighborhood, singing at church, bagging your groceries, cleaning your home, cutting your lawn. Ask God to show you who He is calling you to know in a deeper way.

*Jesus, I want to live the abundant life that You modeled.
Open my eyes to who You are inviting me to know more deeply. Amen.*

WALK INTENTIONALLY.

HABITS FORM US

"All things are lawful for me,"
but not all things are helpful.
"All things are lawful for me,"
but I will not be dominated by anything.
I CORINTHIANS 6:12 ESV

When you think of the word *habits*, what comes to mind? Perhaps it is a sense of shame and failure as you think about the fact that you haven't stepped foot in the gym in months and you are as dehydrated as the Sahara Desert. Maybe you think about those bad habits that have formed in your life like that late-night bowl of ice cream you indulge in daily or the endless scrolling on your phone when you should be going to bed.

The truth is, the word *habits* can bring to mind all sorts of thoughts of what we aren't doing but *should* be doing. It can make us feel defeated thinking that consistency feels like an elusive, out-of-reach pipe dream.

Here's the thing, though: *your life is built upon the habits you do every single day.* Those small, automatic decisions we do without any thinking are making up our lives. And in order to live a life we truly love, we'll spend some time considering these micro-choices we are making without much thought—so that we can begin to be intentional about them.

DAY 71

Think about your "micro-choices." What are the little automatic decisions you make in a day without even thinking about them?

*God, open my eyes to notice the "little things" this week.
Help me to notice how I move through the day
so that I can be intentional about living well. Amen.*

WALK INTENTIONALLY.

PAY ATTENTION

*So then, be careful how you walk,
not as unwise people but as wise.*
EPHESIANS 5:15 NASB

Congrats on making it this far in our journey together. Are you ready to create some new habits? Before we get going on adding new habits, I want you to pay attention to what you are already doing. *Why, you ask? Can't we get started already?*

Well, for one thing, awareness of those automatic behaviors—the ones you've already begun to notice—is key in helping us make new ones and break old ones that aren't serving us well. If you happen to swipe a cookie every time you pass the pantry, that habit will keep you from reaching a goal of losing weight or becoming healthier. If you know that every day you already take your vitamins, that may be a perfect time to add a full eight-ounce cup of water to reach a water goal. It is a hack called habit stacking. But for now, I want you to review exactly what your habits are in a day.

Learning to pay attention to your life, your choices, your everyday decisions is really what makes a difference in stepping fully into a life you love.

The Bible says, "Pay careful attention, then, to how you walk—not as unwise people but as wise" (Ephesians 5:15 CSB). Wise women pay attention to their lives, their thoughts, and their actions. They pay attention to where they are heading and how they are getting there.

DAY 72

Make three lists: Helpful Habits, Harmful Habits, and Halfway Habits. (Imagine "halfway" as those things that are what Paul calls "lawful" but not "helpful.") Then mentally scroll through your daily routine and jot down your regular practices.

God, I thank You for this opportunity I have to be intentional about how I'm living. Continue to open my eyes so that I can make conscious choices toward living a life I love. Amen.

WALK INTENTIONALLY.

BABY STEPS

*Do not be conformed to this world,
but be transformed by the renewal of your mind.*
ROMANS 12:2 ESV

In his book *Atomic Habits*, James Clear shares a story about a cycling team that was really struggling. But when a new coach came in, his strategy was to make everything—from equipment to clothing to performance—1 percent better. Doesn't sound like much, does it? But all those small changes, the baby steps, were what this team needed to become the best in the world.

If I challenged you today to ride your bike two hundred miles to build muscle quickly, you wouldn't improve at all. But if I encourage you to go 1 percent further or 1 percent faster each day, that would result in real improvement for you. What's true of cycling is going to be true of all kinds of habits in your life.

Whatever new habit you decide to build into your life, don't go too big! If you want to increase your hydration, start by adding an extra cup of water to each meal. If you want to spend more time reading, start by aiming for five pages before bedtime each night, not five chapters.

The big habit-making win is counterintuitive, because it's aiming for what's small!

DAY 73

You've already noticed the daily habits that make up your day. What's a small—1 percent!—tweak you could make to one of your existing habits?

_____
_____
_____
_____
_____
_____
_____
_____
_____
_____
_____
_____
_____
_____
_____
_____
_____
_____
_____
_____

*God, I am **all** in to be transformed by You.*
Give me wisdom and courage to take the baby steps I need
to take daily to create healthy habits that contribute to a life I love. Amen.

WALK INTENTIONALLY.

WORK THAT BODY

*Or do you not know that your body
is a temple of the Holy Spirit within you,
whom you have from God?
You are not your own, for you were bought with a price.
So glorify God in your body.*

I CORINTHIANS 6:19-20 ESV

As we begin to be intentional about habit making, I'm wanting you to be really intentional in *four areas*: physical, spiritual, financial, and relational. I chose these four for this journey we're taking together because I know that when one of these is out of whack, it makes it harder to love the life we have. Let's start with the physical.

So, what habit to care for your physical body is going to be most useful for you in this season? Maybe it will be taking that morning walk. Or, if your diet is 80 percent carbs—*I see you*—you may commit to eating one serving of a leafy green veggie every day. It could also be hydration or rest or flexibility or something else. You choose.

Frame this choice as being *kind* to yourself. Make sense? Drinking four more cups of water every day isn't a burden—it's a way to bless your body. Jogging for five minutes and walking for twenty-five isn't a burden—it's a way to bless your body. Because all of our habits *begin in the brain*, I encourage you to think about your new habits as a way to bless your life, bless yourself. You got this, girl!

DAY 74

Don't rush into choosing a new physical habit. Spend some time and ask God two things: *What does my body most need right now? What habit can I establish to bless my body with what it most needs?*

___

*God, I do believe that my body is a temple; it's where **You** live!
Help me to honor You, and me, by establishing
healthy habits that allow me to flourish. Amen.*

> WALK INTENTIONALLY.

LOVE GOD

"Love the Lord your God with all your heart and with all your soul and with all your mind and with all your strength."

MARK 12:30 NIV

When a real smarty-pants know-it-all asked Jesus what the *most most most* important commandment was, Jesus made it really simple for him and for us: *love God*.

To be clear, you were created to be in relationship with God. And if you've let that slide—because you're busy or because you've been lazy or because something bad happened and you're mad at God—I get it. But if that's you, I need you to hear that you're only hurting yourself. You're missing out on a source—on *the* source—of life that really is life.

So this moment, this chance to develop a healthy spiritual habit, is a holy opportunity for you. (*You're welcome.*) And I'm going to encourage you to keep it small. Consider taking one of these baby steps:

- When I wake up, I'll spend ten minutes in silence, just spending time with God, listening.
- Before I drive to work, I'm going to glance at the weekly sticky note I've put on my dash and memorize one verse of Scripture, speaking it aloud and letting it live in my heart.
- At bedtime, I'm going to pull out a pen, open up a fresh journal, and just talk to God by writing words.

When you commit to being with God—in silence, in His Word, in prayer—you invest in what matters most, and you make yourself available to receive God's leading.

DAY 75

Spend time talking to God about what *one thing* is the right spiritual habit to establish today.

God, forgive me for not being more intentional about my relationship with You. There's no way I can create a life worth loving without You. I want You with me in this and in everything. Amen.

WALK INTENTIONALLY.

DAILY BREAD

"Give us this day our daily bread."
MATTHEW 6:11 AMP

Consider two women: One woman inherited millions from her wealthy grandparents, and she can purchase whatever she wants whenever she wants. And *she does*. But she's not living a life she loves. A second woman, without enough money, is worried every single day about how she'll provide for her family. It is *not* a life she loves. I wonder if you see yourself, in some small way, in either one of these women. What I know for sure is that God's heart is for every one of us to have *enough* to meet our needs. When Jesus coaches us how to pray, He calls that "our daily bread." That's what we're invited to ask God for.

As we think about the kinds of habits that allow us to live a life we love, I want you to be really intentional about whatever "bread" God has given you. Specifically, think about how you use what you've been given in three ways: saving, spending, giving. If you're squandering whatever it is God has given you—on homes or cars or impulse buys—develop a habit to save. If you're careless in the ways you spend, develop a habit to help you spend responsibly. And, whether you have a little or a lot, learn to be faithful in *giving* to God and to others.

DAY 76

Spend time talking to God about saving, spending, and giving. Listen with your heart, and let God guide you to one new healthy habit.

Father, You are the giver of all good gifts.
Thank You for being my good provider. Teach me to live well
by creating healthy financial habits. Amen.

WALK INTENTIONALLY.

LOVE PEOPLE

"'Love the Lord your God with all your heart and with all your soul and with all your mind and with all your strength.' The second is this: 'Love your neighbor as yourself.' There is no commandment greater than these."

MARK 12:30-31 NIV

Wait, Chrystal, you shared this verse a few days ago..."

Yes, and...

When the know-it-all asked Jesus what was the *most most most* important thing, he was clearly asking for *one thing*. And I can almost see Jesus raising two fingers in the air to answer the man's question. It was as if Jesus was saying that loving God and loving people can't *not* go together.

If you're serious about discovering the gift of you, I want you to create a habit that supports your relationships. And while there are all kinds of good reasons to invest in relationships with family or girlfriends or mentors or mentees or whoever for this step in the journey, I want you to consider who is the person, or the people, who help you do what Jesus coaches you to do: love God, love people. Maybe it is a mentor of yours, who shepherds you in these ways. Maybe it's someone else. Ask God to open your eyes to a person who's in your life who can join you in pursuit of loving God and loving people.

DAY 77

Who is someone in your life who loves God and loves people? The habit you want to build is to connect, on the regular, with this person. Get specific about what this will look like for you.

_____
_____
_____
_____
_____
_____
_____
_____
_____
_____
_____
_____
_____
_____
_____
_____
_____
_____
_____
_____

Jesus, in Your commands I hear You describing exactly what it looks like to live a life I love because I'm being who God made me to be. Teach me to love You and love others. Amen.

WALK INTENTIONALLY.

POWER OF THE TONGUE

Death and life are in the power of the tongue: and they that love it shall eat the fruit thereof.

PROVERBS 18:21 KJV

"You won't succeed."

"You can't change."

"You're going to blow it."

Has anyone ever said those words to you? *Have you ever said them to yourself?* Proverbs tells us the power of life and death is in the tongue. When you speak negativity, about yourself and others, you are speaking death into circumstances you could speak life into.

Your success at building a life you love is going to be influenced by the words you say to yourself, *in your head*. And the habit I want you to establish—that's like the hydration you want to have on every step of this journey—is to *speak life* with the words you say to yourself.

"You can do all things through Christ who gives you strength."

"God is making you new."

"You can do it."

And I want you to hear that this isn't just some pep talk that won't make a difference. The words you speak—with your lips and also in your heart and mind—make *all* the difference. Choose to speak life, and begin to notice the difference.

Think big picture. Imagine the snapshot of that lovable life you're creating.

DAY 78

First, list the objections you hear in your head, the reasons you won't succeed at creating that life. Then, invite God to help you craft some affirmations that are more true than the lies you've believed.

___

*Lord, I believe You made me to live an abundant life.
Send Your Spirit to guide my heart and mind, that I might speak only
what is good, what is true, what is life-giving. Amen.*

WALK INTENTIONALLY.

MAKE IT STICKY

*Be renewed in the spirit of your minds,
and . . . put on the new self,
created after the likeness of God
in true righteousness and holiness.*

EPHESIANS 4:23-24 ESV

Habits, whether we like it or not, can end up *defining* who we become. They can make us into someone we don't want to be. They can keep us from stepping into who God intends for us to be. But, thanks be to God, we have agency and power to own our lives by changing our habits! That means that our habits can also *make* us into who we want to be and *equip* us to step into who God intends for us to be.

Here's one simple silly pro tip on one way to help habits stick. We agree that our habits all begin in our brains, right? So, I want to encourage you to offer your brain a *cue* that signals the habit you're integrating into your life.

When you implement new habits, you're creating new neural pathways of connection in your brain. To jump-start that process, to make the habit *stick*, I want you to write down the habit you're choosing—drinking eight glasses of water a day, reading for 30 minutes a day, or no alcohol after 8:00 p.m.—on a sticky note and post it somewhere you can see it each day: the bathroom mirror, on your computer, or beside your bed. The more you come back to these thoughts, the more likely you will truly *make the habit stick*.

DAY 79

As you consider the habits you want to implement—physical, spiritual, financial, relational—write them down below and then create and post sticky notes, in just the right spots, as cues to remind you to practice the habits!

_____
_____
_____
_____
_____
_____
_____
_____
_____
_____
_____
_____
_____
_____
_____
_____
_____
_____
_____
_____
_____

God, thank You for being my helper. I am serious about becoming who You made me to be by creating a life that I—and You—love. Give me the courage to walk in these new ways. Amen.

WALK INTENTIONALLY.

SLOW AND STEADY WINS THE RACE

"Do not despise these small beginnings."
ZECHARIAH 4:10 NLT

Slow and steady wins the race.

If you want to win at living a life you love, I encourage you to do it two ways: slow and steady. For example, it may feel impossible to go from drinking hardly any water in a given day to chugging a gallon. But how could you progressively make that habit? You could start with adding one glass a day for a week. Then, start the next week with two glasses. You could keep this going week by week until you reach your goal, and it becomes a daily habitual practice for you.

You can apply this principle to any change you want to make. You might want to spend an hour a day with the Lord in the morning, reading scripture and praying. But currently you're lucky to get five minutes with Him. Start with an easy, achievable amount of time like ten minutes a day for a week. Building upon that is much more likely to help you get to that desired end than trying to start with an hour. *Small, consistent, building of habits* will give you the momentum you want for big, sweeping changes.

DAY 80

Consider the four habits to which you're committing to practice—physical, spiritual, financial, relational—and make sure that you're starting *small*. Then write yourself a reminder—like your own pep talk!—encouraging yourself to be consistent with these changes.

God, give me the grace to be consistent in the choices I'm making to embrace a life that truly is the abundant life you offer. Quicken my mind and strengthen my will so that I will choose consistently for what is best.
Amen.

ACTIVATE PRACTICES.

CREATE SPACE

*When I look at your heavens, the work of your fingers,
the moon and the stars, which you have set in place,
what is man that you are mindful of him,
and the son of man that you care for him?*
PSALM 8:3-4 ESV

Since you're being intentional about creating new life-giving habits, it's worth naming the fact that the old death-dealing ones can be kind of . . . *sticky*. It's how you've always done it, right? But here's the rub: often, in order to do a new thing, you have to create a space where you can envision the new thing, a new space that gets you out of old ways of thinking.

This week, create a space that speaks to you. For me, that "space" is somewhere near water. So sometimes I'll be intentional about sitting by a lake near home. Sometimes I'll sit with a friend talking beside a pool. And sometimes I will create an atmosphere right in home by taking a bath. Being in or around water gives me the space to think beyond what I see or what I've done in the past.

Your space doesn't have to be the ocean. Maybe you will choose to light your favorite candle in a special spot in your home. Or maybe it's a coffee shop that makes room for you to do what the regular everyday stuff won't let you do.

DAY 81

Reflect on the kinds of spaces that are life-giving for you. Consider the experience with all your senses! Then be very specific about how you will choose or create one special space that makes room for you to welcome the new.

*Lord, You fashioned the moon and the stars, the sun and the ocean.
You are the author of beauty, peace, and renewal.
Be with me as I step into the newness You have for me. Amen.*

ACTIVATE PRACTICES.

GIVE THANKS

*Be thankful in all circumstances,
for this is God's will for you who belong to Christ Jesus.*
I THESSALONIANS 5:18 NLT

I'm eager to share some daily life-giving practices that are going to *empower* you to live a life you love. The first is likely intuitive. You've heard it before. But don't neglect it: I'm encouraging you to practice gratitude.

Gratitude at its core is about being thankful, showing appreciation, and finding the good in even the darkest of situations. It is not about attempting to make yourself happy and will not prevent negative thoughts and emotions. However, gratitude does help you have more positive emotions. It will point your thoughts toward the good experiences in your life. And ultimately it has shown to improve health and relationships.

In a *Positive Psychology* study (2005) it was shown that maintaining a gratitude journal lowered depressive symptoms by at least 30 percent. And over time, research suggests practicing gratitude may help train your brain to recognize the positive in negative situations and ultimately improve your mental health. Gratitude even improves the quality of sleep, reduces the amount of time it takes for a person to fall asleep, and increases the amount of time one stays asleep. What does all this mean? When you are grateful, life is better.

DAY 82

I want you to spend time getting really specific about what gratitude looks like *for you*. Create a robust list of all the things for which you're grateful, and then snap a photo of it to keep as your phone wallpaper!

Creator God, thank You for wiring us to thrive when we practice gratitude! Open my eyes to all the goodness in my life. Today I give You thanks as the giver of all good gifts. Amen.

ACTIVATE PRACTICES.

GRATITUDE IN THE MESS

*Why are you in despair, my soul?
And why are you restless within me?
Wait for God, for I will again praise Him
for the help of His presence, my God.*

PSALM 42:5 NASB

There are days when gratitude spills out of us, aren't there? It's the healthy birth of a sibling's child. It's the promotion at work. It's your parents' or grandparents' fiftieth wedding anniversary celebration. *But there are other days . . .* The day of the unexpected diagnosis. The day of declaring bankruptcy. The day of receiving the awful news. It's more than a little difficult on these days to muster even an ounce of gratitude.

But I don't want to let you off the hook. And the reason I don't want to let you off the hook is because of all the research that demonstrates that God wired us to *thrive* when we practice gratitude. It's in our design! So without negating the reality of the challenges you face, I want you to be intentional about practicing gratitude when it's difficult. And I'm not suggesting that you put on a fake smile and pretend either. If you've been awake stressing about finances all night, I'm pushing you to notice the glint of the sunrise outside your window. If you are sharing a friend's heavy burden, invite her over to eat a delicious slice of chocolate cake. Be intentional about choosing gratitude in the midst of your mess.

DAY 83

You've made a big list of things for which you can be grateful. And today I want you to narrow it down to *three core things*. These are the three you can hang onto in your most difficult days.

_____

*God, on my hard days, open my eyes to recognize glimpses of goodness.
Teach me to give You thanks when I'm not feeling it,
knowing as if this is how I was made to flourish. Amen.*

ACTIVATE PRACTICES.

AVOIDING TEMPTATION

"Watch and pray so that you will not fall into temptation. The spirit is willing, but the flesh is weak."
MATTHEW 26:41 NIV

Here's what we know about the brain: *it takes the path of least resistance.* It's why the cookie you can grab and go is an easier choice than pulling out the veggies, washing them, chopping them, and putting them in a to-go bag. It's why you reach for your phone when you have a minute of stillness instead of pulling out your Bible. In some ways, your brain can be a bit lazy and will go for that quick and easy spike of dopamine, that neurotransmitter that can make you feel a moment of pleasure and keeps you motivated, whether toward good or bad choices.

To discover and embrace the gift of you, you don't do yourself any favors if you aren't eliminating the things you naturally gravitate to in stress or without even thinking. If you know those Zapps Jalepeño Chips can't be enjoyed in moderation and you're on track to become a healthier you, why keep buying them? If you see how distracting your phone is when you wake up and it's right next to your bed and it's keeping you from getting into God's Word, why not put it somewhere else? Don't set yourself up for failure before you're even out of the gate.

When you make choices to eliminate the sabotaging decisions *before* you make them, the benefit will be in the progress you see in reaching your goals.

DAY 84

What do you need to do to set yourself up for success? What little change can you make—in advance—to ensure your success?

God, You know my heart. And You know the ways I'm tempted to choose what's easy. Help me to set up my environment for the success I desire. Amen.

ACTIVATE PRACTICES.

DECISION MADE

And let steadfastness have its full effect,
that you may be perfect and complete, lacking in nothing.
JAMES 1:4 ESV

Some of us get all fired up to live differently, often on January 1, and three weeks later we're back to our old bad habits. It's "the drift." We fail to follow through on the decision we made. And now we know why, right? We know it's because the brain naturally chooses the path of least resistance. So we're taking the steps now to accomplish our goals: by creating a space for change, by expressing gratitude, by avoiding temptation. These are the practical steps we can take to create a life we love.

I want to offer one more. Living the life we love requires *consistency* (I know, I know, it's not sexy, but it's true!) When we're consistent, we keep choosing, again and again, day after day, to honor the decision we've made. When we make the decision to read one psalm every night but we're exhausted, we splash some cold water on our faces and keep reading. When we purpose to drink eight glasses of water a day, we start as soon as we wake up. When we have decided to learn a new skill, we practice it daily, whether we feel like it or not. Being consistent—especially when we don't feel like it—is the secret to reaching the finish line.

DAY 85

Get specific about what *consistency* looks like in your life. List the little choices—that you may have neglected in the past—that will help you to be consistent.

_____
_____
_____
_____
_____
_____
_____
_____
_____
_____
_____
_____
_____
_____
_____
_____
_____
_____
_____
_____
_____
_____

God, You know how I'm tempted to do what's easiest. But what I want even more than that is to succeed *at creating a life I love. Help me to be disciplined to make the right choices. Amen.*

ACTIVATE PRACTICES.

DECIDE ONCE

*May he grant you your heart's desire
and fulfill all your plans!*

PSALM 20:4 ESV

Let's dish about one-time decisions that will *help you* in your quest to make habits that stick. One-time decisions are those choices you make *once* in an effort to help you along the way in becoming a person who *does* what you are setting out to do. They can sometimes require a bit of a bigger investment in order to reach your goals, but they can help you move further down the path you are setting out on.

If you're working on the habit of going to bed by ten every night, you might decide you need to invest in a better mattress to help you get the sleep you need. If you're trying to lose weight, you might join the gym that offers free personal trainers. If you are working on that book, it might be time to buy that computer you've been eyeing. It could even be as easy as picking out the best workout outfit Target has to offer so that you always *know* what you'll be wearing to the gym or buying that nice tumbler that keeps your water super cold so you will be encouraged to drink more.

As you think about your habits, is there a one-time decision you can make to help you move forward in your goals?

DAY 86

Think of one or two one-time decisions you would like to make to help you in your habits. Even if you can't make that decision now, start working toward it. What could you cut out (*hey, $6 daily Starbucks runs!*) in order to invest down the road?

_____
_____
_____
_____
_____
_____
_____
_____
_____
_____
_____
_____
_____
_____
_____
_____
_____
_____
_____
_____

Father, You are the giver of all good gifts.
Thank You for being my good provider.
Teach me to live well by creating healthy financial habits. Amen.

ACTIVATE PRACTICES.

CHOOSE JOY ON THE JOURNEY

Always be full of joy in the Lord.
I say it again—rejoice!
PHILIPPIANS 4:4 NLT

As Paul addresses the church of Philippi, he tells them to "always be full of joy in the Lord." Yet, here's the thing: research shows your brain cannot handle both negative and positive emotions at the same time. This means that if you're going to be filled with joy, you have to make space for it by releasing the negative. How do we do this?

Paul teaches that through prayer you should submit the negative to God so that you can experience His peace. He instructs the church to pray about everything (Philippians 4:6) and to not be filled with negativity. You have to give your negative thoughts, tendencies, and emotions to the Lord. Ask Him to turn your gaze toward all-things life-giving. Memorize Scripture and when you hear those negative thoughts in your mind, recall His Word and focus on His goodness.

Friend, this is your opportunity to set yourself free from the captivity of negativity.

DAY 87

Notice what occupies your mind. Specifically, list five things that you can be tempted to dwell on that are negative. Then, brainstorm five ways to replace those negative thoughts with what is *more true* than the negative.

_____
_____
_____
_____
_____
_____
_____
_____
_____
_____
_____
_____
_____
_____
_____
_____
_____
_____
_____
_____
_____
_____

*Father God, thank You for creating me with the ability
to be set free from negativity! Your design is amazing.
Give me the wisdom to notice my thoughts and to choose joy. Amen.*

ACTIVATE PRACTICES.

CHOOSE WHAT IS GOOD

Fix your thoughts on what is true, and honorable, and right, and pure, and lovely, and admirable. Think about things that are excellent and worthy of praise.

PHILIPPIANS 4:8 NLT

Now that you know the secret to being set free from negativity, I want us to go even bigger! One of my favorite books is *Anatomy of the Soul* by Curt Thompson. Thompson reminds us that "Even though you cannot change the events of your story, you can change the way you experience your story." Choosing to release the negative is half of the process. Now you have to choose to *find and focus on the good*.

You cannot guarantee only good experiences and people in your life, but you can choose to only hold on to the good that exists within the negative experiences and people. You control how you react to everything you encounter. You control whether you walk away with anger and frustration or whether you grow and learn. You control whether or not you intentionally look to find beauty in all things. The trajectory of your days will depend on what you choose to do with your thoughts and reactions each day.

Today, as you think about the hard circumstances and people you may be dealing with, I pray you will find the needed grace, find gratitude, and choose to focus on what is lovely in those spaces.

DAY 88

Pause to look at the circumstance or person in your life today that is difficult. Then invite God's Spirit to show you what is true, honorable, right, pure, lovely, and admirable. (If you struggle, stick with it. It's worth it.)

God, today I choose to set my mind on what is worthy and true. In the parts of my story that are tricky right now, help me to see what is good. Amen.

ACTIVATE PRACTICES.

LET SOMEONE KNOW

I thank my God upon every remembrance of you.
PHILIPPIANS 1:3 KJV

As we are being intentional about embracing who God made you to be, you know that I want you to be purposeful about investing in the relationships that are important to you. And a really practical way to live that out is to let one of these special people know what they mean to you.

Maybe a friend was a steadfast support to you when you went through your divorce. Maybe a family member lent you money when you needed it most. Maybe a childhood friend walked with you during a season of mental health struggles. Does that person know how much their support meant to you?

You may feel grateful to them, but gratitude left unspoken is gratitude wasted. Yes, feel grateful, but also verbalize how you feel with others. Your assignment today is to not only be grateful but also to share your words of appreciation for someone by writing them a thank you note. It doesn't have to be lengthy; it can simply be a couple of sentences expressing how much you value their presence in your space.

DAY 89

Make a robust list of those who have been a gift to you on your journey. Then, write a note of thanks to *one*. (And there is guaranteed goodness if you choose to eventually make it through the whole list!)

_____
_____
_____
_____
_____
_____
_____
_____
_____
_____
_____
_____
_____
_____
_____
_____
_____
_____
_____
_____
_____

*God, You've taught me that my life is better when I practice gratitude.
So I give You thanks for these people You've placed in my life,
and I commit to sharing that gratitude with them. Amen.*

| ACTIVATE PRACTICES. |

YOU ARE HIS

*Acknowledge that the L<small>ORD</small> is God!
He made us, and we are His.*
PSALM 100:3 NLT

Listen, I live a very real and full life. I know how easy it is to be consumed by "all the things": the chores, the bills, and the strained relationships. I get it. *But you don't have to stay stuck there!*

I'm really excited about this final activation, because it is *foundational*. It's something that you can do daily and reap the benefits. Today I'm encouraging you to meditate on being grateful for that which is bigger than you. The psalmist announces, "Acknowledge that the L<small>ORD</small> is God! He made us, and we are His." Every day we can choose to set our minds on what is most true about who God is and who we are. Say it with me: *He made me, and I am His.*

We belong to God. He loves us. No matter what is swirling around us or even within us, we can be grateful for *who* we are and *whose* we are. *We are His image bearers, and He loves us.*

Friend, I *know* there's still work to be done. You may need to go back to school. You may need to finish that project at home. You may need to refocus on your weight loss plan. Whatever the thing is you keep telling yourself is making you less than . . . it's not. Know that there is nothing you can or cannot do to change the essence of who you are, and that is a reason to be grateful.

DAY 90

Spend time meditating on the radical truth that God made you and you are His. Reflect on what that means, and then get specific about what it means for you in your circumstance *right now*.

_____
_____
_____
_____
_____
_____
_____
_____
_____
_____
_____
_____
_____
_____
_____
_____
_____
_____
_____
_____
_____
_____

Lord, I acknowledge that You are God!
And in the nitty-gritty of my daily life, that reality changes things.
I rejoice that I am Yours. Amen

CONTINUE GROWING.

SHOW UP

*Beloved, if God so loved us,
we also ought to love one another.*
1 JOHN 4:11 ESV

Here's a secret that might feel counterintuitive at first: discovering the gift of you isn't all about you. Well, it is, and it isn't . . .

I know you've had those days that are long and hard and exhausting. There's nothing you can skip, and so you soldier on. And when the finish line is in sight, there's one more thing on your calendar. I had one of those days awhile back, and I was whooped. But friends of my parents were celebrating a special event, so I dragged myself back to the car, drove farther than I would have chosen, and showed up. When the woman in this couple laid eyes on me, her joy was palpable as she exclaimed, "We're so glad you came! It's so good to see you!"

The fact is, because we like to curl up on the couch watching Netflix at night, we lie to ourselves. We convince ourselves, "It doesn't matter that much," or "I'll do it later." Whether it's showing up at the event or sending the card or making the phone call, we put it off. Sometimes forever.

So let me ask you a question. What do you know that you should do but haven't done? And, specifically, how can you bless someone else with who you are?

DAY 91

Consider the people in your life, and recall the ways you've intended to support them but haven't followed through: the text, the call, the note, the visit. Then choose one you'll execute this week.

*God, I confess that living a life
that's all about me isn't Your best for me.
Open my eyes and ears to how You're inviting me to be **for** others. Amen*

CONTINUE GROWING.

KEEP SHOWING UP

"Have I not commanded you?
Be strong and courageous.
Do not be frightened, and do not be dismayed,
for the LORD your God is with you wherever you go."
JOSHUA 1:9 ESV

As I was graduating from college with my accounting degree, I had the privilege of working for one of the big six accounting firms in the country. During orientation, one of the African American partners spoke to those of us who were also black and brown. He said, "Here's how I made it: I showed up every day." He continued on to say that before getting out of the car each day to walk in the door, he'd played the song "Eye of the Tiger" from the movie *Rocky*. He was his own hype man. He kept showing up.

The lesson stuck with me, and when my own son was working a job he didn't love, I hyped him up! "Your boss may not be making your life easy right now, but be that young man you were made to be." Then I taught him how to hype himself up, how to be his own hype man!

One of the secrets to building this life you love is to keep showing up. Show up for yourself. Show up for others. And sometimes, in order to show up, you've gotta be your own hype girl. To create a life you love, keep showing up.

DAY 92

Learn to hype yourself up, and get creative with it. What's the *song* that fuels you to do the hard thing? What's the *mantra* that gives you extra courage? What's the *Scripture* that strengthens you in hard moments?

Father God, I know that—with You—I can do hard things. Equip me to keep showing up. Fill my heart and mind with what I need to thrive. Amen.

CONTINUE GROWING.

WALK WITH A FRIEND

*The righteous choose their friends carefully,
but the way of the wicked leads them astray.*
PROVERBS 12:26 NIV

You and I have been walking this path together, but as we prepare to go our separate ways, I encourage you to welcome a friend to support you as you purpose to continue living well. And you can discern who that friend might be from a few key passages in Proverbs. Proverbs are like wise "tweets" that give practical wisdom for how to live. They are truths that can guide you into a righteous life. And this book of the Bible has a lot to say about finding—and being—a good friend. These four verses give you clues about what you want to find in a friend:

- *A friend loves at all times, and a brother [or a sister] is born for a time of adversity.* Proverbs 17:17 NIV
- *One who has unreliable friends soon comes to ruin, but there is a friend who sticks closer than a brother.* Proverbs 18:24 NIV
- *Walk with the wise and become wise, for a companion of fools suffers harm.* Proverbs 13:20 NIV
- *The righteous choose their friends carefully, but the way of the wicked leads them astray.* Proverbs 12:26 NIV

Who is the friend who's supported you during tough times? Who has been consistently reliable? Who has demonstrated wisdom? Who practices righteousness? If you have a friend who checks these boxes, recruit her to be on your team!

DAY 93

Write out the four passages referenced in today's devotion from Proverbs, and reflect on who in your life embodies these qualities. Then, be intentional to share with her your intention to discover—and embrace—the gift of you. Help her know how she can

_____
_____
_____
_____
_____
_____
_____
_____
_____
_____
_____
_____
_____
_____
_____
_____
_____
_____
_____
_____
_____
support you.

God, thank You for your Word that guides me in the way I should go. Open my eyes to the friend who can join me on this journey. And teach me how to love her well. Amen.

CONTINUE GROWING.

EXERCISE DISCIPLINE

For the moment all discipline seems painful rather than pleasant, but later it yields the peaceful fruit of righteousness to those who have been trained by it.

HEBREWS 12:11 ESV

Whether it's because we didn't like being disciplined as children, we feel too tired to be disciplined as adults, "discipline" can often feel hard to muster. But it matters on this journey because it's what keeps us going.

If you identify as being "not disciplined," that simply means that you don't *feel* like doing it. And the only difference between you and the person who does the thing is that they *decided* to do it and they followed through to do it. Discipline is what you do.

And because I'm all about the solutions, I'm encouraging you to set yourself up for success. Put your clothes out for the morning gym routine at bedtime. Spend a few hours Sunday afternoon prepping healthy meals for the week. Ask a friend to be your walking buddy. When you build structures of accountability around you, it makes it easier to show up and do the thing you don't want to do. Discipline is the habit of acting in the moment based on a decision you made in advance, regardless of your current feelings. So show up and do the thing.

DAY 94

You know the weak spot in your life where you fail, on the regular, to exercise discipline. Today's the day you decide to follow through on your decision. Spend time journaling about how you can build structures to support your commitment to discipline.

*God, I need Your help. I have a history of slacking in this area,
but I know that You want to be my Helper.
Give me the courage to act on the decisions I've made. Amen.*

CONTINUE GROWING.

EMPOWERED BY GOD

For God has not given us a spirit of fear and timidity, but of power, love, and self-discipline.

II TIMOTHY 1:7 NLT

Because it's *sooo* important and so key in embracing the gift of who we are, I don't want us to skip past self-discipline too quickly. Self-discipline can feel like something that certain people just have an extra dose of when it comes to living out their lives. That is not true.

Scripture tells us that self-discipline isn't just some conjuring up of the will. It's something God gives us to fulfill what He is calling us to. In II Timothy 1:7, Paul says, "For God has not given us a spirit of fear and timidity, but of power, love, and self-discipline." This means you have access to more power than you might realize. Through the Holy Spirit, we possess a power to move in such a way that we aren't controlled by our unhealthy desires that want to keep us in bondage; rather, we can push past them into living freely on the path God has set before us.

Today, where would you like to see that power at work in your life?

DAY 95

Spend time reflecting on the shift toward being filled by the power and discipline that God offers you. Pray to the Lord for the strength to press past your fears and into a life that is shaped by Spirit-led self-control.

_____
_____
_____
_____
_____
_____
_____
_____
_____
_____
_____
_____
_____
_____
_____
_____
_____
_____
_____
_____

God, You know that I need You, and I know that I need You.
Send Your Spirit to fill me with the power You promise. Amen.

CONTINUE GROWING.

CHOOSE TO HOPE

May the God of hope fill you with all joy and peace in believing, so that by the power of the Holy Spirit you may abound in hope.

ROMANS 15:13 ESV

"Things will never change."

"I will never change."

"My life will never change."

As you're getting near the finish line of our journey together—and as you *continue* to live into the gift of you—I want to remind you that the key is that it begins in your mind. When you have a growth mindset, you are able to say, "Things can change; I can change; life can change." No matter where you are today, believe that you can learn to thrive despite where you are right now.

We've been heading toward you embracing the gift of you, and just as it is in our relationships with people, it's a *choice*. Yes, you can feel it, but discovering the gift you are is something that you can *do*. Have a growth mindset. You are a daughter of the King and your Father has a plan for you. However, you have to participate in that plan. As you march on, I want you to choose the life you love daily by affirming:

"Things can change; I can change; life can change."

DAY 96

In your time of reflection, write the three mantras on the previous page. And then, employing a growth mindset, add your own personal affirmations to these!

Lord, I am leaving the past in the past.
When I think of what You have for me today and tomorrow and the next day, I do believe that with You I can create a life I love. Amen.

CONTINUE GROWING.

RECEIVE GRACE

*But he gives more grace. Therefore it says,
"God opposes the proud but gives grace to the humble."*

JAMES 4:6 ESV

"Give yourself grace" has become a popular mantra to say to friends who are bearing a heavy load. When our girlfriends are crushed at work or overwhelmed at home or struggling in school, we encourage them to be patient and kind *to themselves*. We coach them to give themselves *grace*.

This is the posture I want you to have as you continue this journey. I want you to be generous in offering *yourself* grace. (Truly! Be as kind to yourself as you would be to your girlfriend.)

If you don't walk this path with grace for yourself, you're going to burn out. Because the reality is that there *will* be bumps along the way. You'll lose steam. You'll poop out. You'll do the thing you swore you wouldn't do. And then what? *Then*, you stand back up, brush the dirt off, and keep going.

Yes, I want you to keep going. Like Dori from the movie "Nemo," just keep swimming. But I also want you to be abundantly kind and gracious to yourself on this journey.

DAY 97

Consider the words you'd say to a friend who yelled at her kid, unintentionally regained the weight she lost, lost her job, found herself in debt, or found herself in the middle of a divorce. If you loved her, you'd be *gentle* with her even if she felt like she was failing to run her race well. Love yourself well. Spend time writing gentle affirmations of kindness to *yourself*, to return to when you find yourself struggling to win.

_____
_____
_____
_____
_____
_____
_____
_____
_____
_____
_____
_____
_____
_____
_____

God, thank You for kindness and gentleness on this journey.
Whenever I need it, You give me more grace.
Teach me to be as kind to myself as You are to me. Amen.

CONTINUE GROWING.

EYES ON THE PRIZE

*But our citizenship is in heaven.
And we eagerly await a Savior from there,
the Lord Jesus Christ.*

PHILIPPIANS 3:20 NIV

What we've been about on this journey is being intentional about discovering the gift of you—a life in which you're flourishing physically, socially, emotionally, and spiritually. And I think you know by now that I believe you were made for what Paul calls "life that is truly life" (I Timothy 6:19 NIV). Whatever your life looks like today, you know how very passionate I am about the power you have to create a life that you love. And I am so proud of the hard work and effort you put into this process.

But it is also my great delight to announce that this life is not all there is. So I want you to take some time to sit with your creator. Philippians 3:20 (NLT) reminds us that "we are citizens of heaven, where the Lord Jesus Christ lives. And we are eagerly waiting for Him to return as our Savior." You see, friend, as children of God, we will spend eternity with Him. So as we work to build a life we love, here and now, we have the confidence that there is more.

Today, pause to remember the depth of God's love for you and be grateful your eternal future is with Him.

DAY 98

The physical, social, emotional, and spiritual challenges you face now are real. As you spend time with God, reflect both on the depth of His big love for you and also the full redemption—of all the things—that you'll experience in heaven.

*God, I thank You that I have peace that my future is with You.
I believe that You made me and that I belong to You.
Thank You for the confidence that, in Christ, I belong to You. Amen.*

CONTINUE GROWING.

EMBRACE THE GIFT OF *YOU*

And God saw everything that he had made, and behold, it was very good.

GENESIS 1:31 ESV

So my friend, you've been doing the work. You've purposed to discover the gift of you, and now I want you to *live it*! I want you to savor it. To enjoy it. You've done the work. And so I'm giving you permission to not feel like you always have to be reaching for the next thing.

A few years back, in a conversation with my mom and sister, my mom commented, "Find one thing you like, that makes you feel joy, and then camp out there." (Mic drop.)

For my mom, one of those things that brought her joy was watching sunsets. Truly, she *loved* them. So she'd hustle home from errands to get home in time for the sunset and even snap pictures. She'd tell you that she enjoyed the simple things in life.

So, in her memory, I'm giving you permission to enjoy the simple things. Savor the life you have. Appreciate it. Yes, you've still got to be consistent in the decisions you've made, but I also want you to smell the flowers along the way. Hear the birds chirping. And see the sunsets.

DAY 99

What is it that makes you feel joy? What does it look like for you to camp out there? What small decisions can you make to choose to savor the life you have?

*Lord, everything You have made is good.
Give me eyes to see Your goodness.
Teach me to pause to notice and love this life I'm living. Amen.*

CONTINUE GROWING.

JUST KEEP SWIMMING

*A man's mind plans his way
[as he journeys through life],
but the L<small>ORD</small> directs his steps
and establishes them.*

PROVERBS 16:9 AMP

Remember the movie *Finding Nemo*? The spacey fish named Dory repeats to herself, "Just keep swimming, just keep swimming . . ." Well my friend, this is the moment for you to keep swimming!

It's easy to get to the end of an experience like this and think the work is over, but just because we aren't taking the time to do this together, it doesn't mean you are finished! You get the opportunity to take what you've learned and create more and more habits that stick in your life. You get to continue those small, incremental investments in *you* because you are worth it! The process of becoming all God intended for you to be is ongoing, so keep coming back to what you've learned. Let it soak in.

You may need to go back through this material and slow it down and really take it all in. You might want to refresh on certain things we talked about. While today marks the official end to our journey, it is a new beginning in yours.

Don't let those old patterns of belief or those pesky temptations disrupt the progress you've made. *Keep swimming.* Purpose daily to embrace the gift of you.

DAY 100

Think forward, and consider your life one year from now. Describe what you see, and be specific. What will make you happy about how you lived? Determine to continue walking through this life living intentionally but also intentionally taking in the scenery and savoring the moments. After all this is your only one and very precious life.

_____
_____
_____
_____
_____
_____
_____
_____
_____
_____
_____
_____
_____
_____
_____
_____
_____
_____
_____
_____

God, I believe that You are the One who has ordered my steps.
Thank You for joining me on this journey.
Hold me close as I continue to walk with You! Amen.

YOU'VE GOT THIS

You did it! You did the work and completed these one hundred days. I'm so proud of you.

You've discovered the gift of you.

Over these one hundred days, you've done the work to notice where you've been through the years and where you were when you started this journey. You've decided what you want and who you want to be, and now you've got a few more tools in your toolbox that will equip you to live well, to be the girl God made you to be.

Keep this journal in a place where you can return to it, whenever you need a refresher. And know that as you continue to walk this out, to embrace the gift of you, I am cheering you on.

There is no one else like you. You are a one-of-a-kind gift from God to the world. So keep living into that reality every day.

You've Got This,

Chrystal

CHRYSTAL EVANS HURST is the bestselling author of *She's Still There*, *Kingdom Woman*, *Show Up for Your Life*, and *The 28-Day Prayer Journey*. She reaches a wide audience speaking at conferences, sharing on her blog and podcast, and teaching and leading women in her home church.

Chrystal is an energetic, life-loving "girl-next-door" who loves encouraging others to fulfill their potential. With humor and vulnerability, Chrystal tells-it-like-it-is but does so with grace, integrity, and love.

In addition to her work and ministry, Chrystal is a COO (Chief Operating Officer), cultivating hearts and commanding chaos at home. She is a wife, mother of five, and grandmother of five. You can find Chrystal and the chronicles of her life at chrystalevanshurst.com

Dear Friend,

    This book was prayerfully crafted with you, the reader, in mind. Every word, every sentence, every page was thoughtfully written, designed, and packaged to encourage you—right where you are this very moment. At DaySpring, our vision is to see every person experience the life-changing message of God's love. So, as we worked through rough drafts, design changes, edits, and details, we prayed for you to deeply experience His unfailing love, indescribable peace, and pure joy. It is our sincere hope that through these Truth-filled pages your heart will be blessed, knowing that God cares about you—your desires and disappointments, your challenges and dreams.

    He knows. He cares. He loves you unconditionally.

BLESSINGS!
THE DAYSPRING BOOK TEAM

Additional copies of this book and
other DaySpring titles can be purchased
at fine retailers everywhere.
Order online at dayspring.com
or
by phone at 1-877-751-4347